Far Off Things

Other books by Arthur Machen

Novels
  The Hill of Dreams
  The Great Return
  The Terror
  The Secret Glory
  The Green Round
  The Great God Pan
  Kings of Horror
  The Chronicle of Clemendy
  The Great God Pan and The Inmost Light
  The Three Imposters
  The House of Souls
  The Angels of Mons, The Bowmen,
        and Other Legends of the War
  Fantastic Tales or the Way to Attain
  The Shining Pyramid
  The Glorious Mystery
  Ornaments in Jade
  The Children of the Pool and Other Stories
  The Cozy Room and Other Stories
  Holy Terrors
  Tales of Horror and the Supernatural
  Tales of Horror and the Supernatural Volume Two
  The Strange World of Arthur Machen
  Black Crusade
  The Novel of the Black Seal and Other Stories
  The Novel of the White Powder and Other Stories

Far Off Things

ARTHUR MACHEN

ÆGYPAN PRESS

"Far Off Things" was written in 1915, and, the work not being of an encyclopædic nature, no effort has been made to bring it up to date.

The book called "The Anatomy of Tankards" in the text was called in fact "The Anatomy of Tobacco." Simple-hearted American collectors are now willing to give four pounds for a copy of it.

Special thanks to Malcolm Farmer, Katherine Becker, and the Online Distributed Proofreading Team (which can be found at http://www.pgdp.net). Thanks also to The Internet Archive/Canadian Libraries.

1922

Far Off Things
A publication of
ÆGYPAN PRESS

www.aegypan.com

DEDICATION

To Alfred Turner

This is a book, my dear Turner, which I had in my heart to write for many years. The thought of it came to me with that other thought that I was growing — rather, grown — old; that the curtain had definitely been rung down on all the days of my youth. And so I got into the way of looking back, of recalling the far gone times and suns of the 'seventies and early 'eighties when the scene of my life was being set. I made up my mind that I would write about it all — some day.

Some day would undoubtedly have been Never, if it had not been for you. I had not spoken of the projected book to you or anyone else; but one fine morning in 1915 you ordered me to write it! You were then, you will remember, editing the London Evening News, and as a reporter on your staff I had nothing to do but to obey. The book was written, appeared in the paper as "The Confessions of a Literary Man," and now reappears as "Far Off Things."

So far, good. I enjoyed writing the book enormously; and, I frankly confess, I enjoy reading it. In a word, I am not grumbling. But there is one little point that I do not mean to neglect. My complacent views as to "Far Off Things" may not be shared by other and, possibly, more competent judges. And what I want to impress on you is this: that if there is to be trouble, "you are going to have your share of it." You ordered the book to be written, you printed it in your paper, you have urged me to reprint it, not once or twice, but again and again.

Now, you remember Johnson on advising an author to print his book. "This author," said the Doctor, "when mankind are hunting him with a canister at his tail can say, 'I would not have published, had not Johnson, or Reynolds, or Musgrave, or some other good judge commended the work!'"

Now you see the purpose of this Epistle Dedicatory. It is to make it quite clear that, if there is to be any talk of canisters and tails, the order will run:

"Canisters for two!"

ARTHUR MACHEN

Chapter I

One night a year or so ago I was the guest of a famous literary society. This society, or club, it is well known, believes in celebrating literature — and all sorts of other things — in a thoroughly agreeable and human fashion. It meets not in any gloomy hall or lecture room, it has no gritty apparatus of blackboard, chalk, and bleared water-bottle. It summons its members and its guests to a well-known restaurant of the West End, it gives them red and white roses for their buttonholes, and sets them down to an excellent dinner and good red wine at a gaily decked table, flower garlanded, luminous with many starry lamps.

Well, as I say, I found myself on a certain night a partaker of all this cheerfulness. I was one guest among many; there were explorers and ambassadors and great scientific personages and judges, and the author who has given the world the best laughter that it has enjoyed since Dickens died: in a word, I was in much more distinguished company than that to which I am accustomed. And after dinner the Persians (as I will call them) have a kindly and courteous custom of praising their guests; and to my astonishment and delight the

speaker brought me into his oration and said the
kindest and most glowing things imaginable about a
translation I once made of the "Heptameron" of Mar-
garet of Navarre. I was heartily pleased; I hold with
Foker in "Pendennis" that every fellow likes a hand.
Praise is grateful, especially when there has not been
too much of it; but it is not to record my self-compla-
cence that I have told this incident of the Persian
banquet. As I sat at the board and heard the speaker's
kindly compliments, I was visited for a twinkling part
of a moment by a vision; by such a vision as they say
comes to the spiritual eyes of drowning men as they
sink through the green water. The scene about me was
such as one will find nowhere else but in London. The
multitude of lights, the decoration of the great room
and the tables, above all the nature of the company
and something in the very air of the place; all these
were metropolitan in the sense in which the word is
opposed to provincial. This is a subtlety which the
provinces cannot understand, and it is natural enough
that they are unable to do so. The big town in the
Midlands or the North will tell you of its picture
galleries, of its classical concerts, and of the serious
books taken out in great numbers from its flourishing
free libraries. It does not see, and, probably, will never
see, that none of these things is to the point.

Well, from the heart of this London atmosphere I
was suddenly transported in my vision to a darkling,
solitary country lane as the dusk of a November evening closed upon it thirty long years before. And, as I
think that the pure provincial can never understand
the quiddity or essence of London, so I believe that for
the born Londoner the country ever remains an incredible mystery. He knows that it is there — somewhere —
but he has no true vision of it. In spite of himself he
Londonizes it, suburbanizes it; he sticks a gas lamp or

two in the lanes, dots some largish villas of red brick beside them, and extends the District or the Metropolitan to within easy distance of the dark wood. But here was I carried from luminous Oxford Street to the old deep lane in Gwent, which is on the borders of Wales. Nothing that a Londoner would call a town within eight miles, deep silence, deep stillness everywhere; hills and dark wintry woods growing dim in the twilight, the mountain to the west a vague, huge mass against a faint afterlight of the dead day, grey and heavy clouds massed over all the sky. I saw myself, a lad of twenty-one or thereabouts, strolling along this solitary lane on a daily errand, bound for a point about a mile from the rectory. Here a footpath over the fields crossed the road, and by the stile I would wait for the postman. I would hear him coming from far away, for he blew a horn as he walked, so that people in the scattered farms might come out with their letters if they had any. I lounged on the stile and waited, and when the postman came I would give him my packet — the day's portion of "copy" of that Heptameron translation that I was then making and sending to the publisher in York Street, Covent Garden. The postman would put the parcel in his bag, cross the road, and go striding off into the dim country beyond, finding his way on a track that no townsman could see, by field and wood and marshy places, crossing the Canthwr brook by a narrow plank, coming out somewhere on the Llanfrechfa road, and so entering at last Caerleon-on-Usk, the little silent, deserted village that was once the golden Isca of the Roman legions, that is golden forever and immortal in the romances of King Arthur and the Graal and the Round Table.

So, in an instant's time, I journeyed from the lighted room in the big Oxford Street restaurant to the darkening lane in faraway Gwent, in faraway years. I gathered anew for that little while the savor of the autumnal wood beside which the boy of thirty years before was walking, and also the savor of his long-forgotten labors, of his old dreams of life and of letters. The speech and the dream came to an end: and the man on the other side of the table, who is probably the most skillful and witty writer of musical comedy "lyrics" in England, was saying that once on a time he had tried to write real poetry.

I shall always esteem it as the greatest piece of fortune that has fallen to me, that I was born in that noble, fallen Caerleon-on-Usk, in the heart of Gwent. My greatest fortune, I mean, from that point of view which I now more especially have in mind, the career of letters. For the older I grow the more firmly am I convinced that anything which I may have accomplished in literature is due to the fact that when my eyes were first opened in earliest childhood they had before them the vision of an enchanted land. As soon as I saw anything I saw Twyn Barlwm, that mystic tumulus, the memorial of peoples that dwelt in that region before the Celts left the Land of Summer. This guarded the southern limit of the great mountain wall in the west; a little northward was Mynydd Maen — the Mountain of the Stone — a giant, rounded billow; and still to the north mountains, and on fair, clear days one could see the pointed summit of the Holy Mountain by Abergavenny. It would shine, I remember, a pure blue in the far sunshine; it was a mountain peak in a fairy tale. And then to eastward the bedroom window of Llanddewi Rectory looked over hill and valley, over high woods, quivering with leafage like the beloved Zacynthus of Ulysses, away to the forest of Wentwood, to the church tower on the hill above Caerleon. Through a cleft one might see now and again a bright yellow glint of the Severn Sea, and the cliffs of Somerset beyond. And hardly a house in sight in all the landscape, look where you would. Here the gable of a barn, here a glint of a whitewashed farmhouse, here blue wood smoke rising from an orchard grove, where an old cottage was snugly hidden; but only so much if you knew where to look. And of nights, when the dusk fell and the farmer went his rounds, you might chance to see his lantern glimmering a very spark on the hillside. This was all that showed in a vague, dark world; and the only sounds were the faint distant barking of the sheepdog and the melancholy cry of the owls from the border of the brake.

I believe that I have seen at all events the main streets of London at every hour of the day and night. I have viewed, for example, Leicester Square between four and five of a summer morning, and have marveled at its dismal disarray and quite miserable shabbiness of aspect. With the pure morning sun shining upon its gay places in clear splendor they are infinitely more "shocking" than they can appear at night-time to the narrowest of provincials. The Strand is a solemn street at two in the morning, Holborn has a certain vastness and windiness about it as the sky grows from black to grey, and at six the residential quarters seem full of houses of mourning, their white blinds most strictly drawn.

And at one time I had almost as full a knowledge of my native country, though not so much with respect to the category of time as to that of place. I have, it is true, seen the sky above the dark stretch of Wentwood Forest redden to the dawn, and I have lost my way and strayed in a very maze of unknown brooks and hills and woods and wild lands in the blackest hours after midnight. But the habits of the country, unlike those of London, generally fail to give reason or excuse for night wanderings. If you stayed in friendly and hospitable company much after ten of the night, it was usually a case of the spare room, newly aired sheets, one pipe more, and so to bed. This at all events on nights that were very black or tempestuous with wind and rain; for on such nights it is difficult to make out the faint footpath from stile to stile, and only the surest sense of locality will enable one to strike the felled tree or the narrow plank that, hidden by a dense growth of alders, crosses the winding of the brook. But from very early years indeed I became an enchanted student of the daylight country, which, I think, for me never was illuminated by common daylight, but rather by suns that rose from the holy seas of færy and sank down behind magic hills. I was an only child, and as soon as I could walk beyond the limits of the fields and orchards about the rectory, my father would take me with him on such parish visitations as were fairly within the stretch and strength of short legs. Indeed, I began my peregrinations at a still earlier period, for I can remember a visit to the mill, that was paid when I was a passenger in a perambulator, and aged, I suppose, about three.

Later these travels became more frequent, and I have recollections, still fresh and pleasant, of sitting still in old farmhouse kitchens while my father was about his ghostly business. Always, even in the full blaze of summer, there would be a glint of fire on the cavernous hearth and a faint blue spire of wood smoke mounting the huge hollow of the chimney. The smell of this wood smoke scented and sweetened the air, in which there was usually a hint of apples stored away in loft or cellar, somewhere behind one or other of the black tarred doors that opened from every wall in the long, low room, and here and there beveled what should have been an angle. By the hearth stood a big curving settle on one side, on the other there was usually an armchair for the farmer's wife. One small window, with square leaded panes, with solid oaken mullions, looked out on the garden, and so thick were the walls — they were always heavily "battered," or sloped outward towards the ground — that there was a depth of at least three feet between the windowpanes and the inner wall of the room. There was whitewash within and without, renewed every spring, and it is one of the most beautiful circumstances in Gwent that this custom of whitewash prevails. To look up to a mountain side and to see the pure white of the walls of the farms and cottages established there, fronting great winds, but nestling too in a shelter of tossing trees, gives me even now the keenest pleasure. And if on a summer day one climbs up amidst those brave winds and looks down on all the rolling land of Gwent, it is dotted with these white farms, that shine radiant in the sunlight.

And these farmhouse kitchens were floored with stone, which was so purely and exquisitely kept that people said "one could eat bread and butter off Mrs. Morgan's kitchen floor." Such a place was, and still is, my notion of comfort, of the material surroundings which are fit to house a man. Now and then, in these later days, my business — never my pleasure — calls me to our Hôtel Glorieux or our Hôtel Splendide; to the places where the rooms are fifty feet high, where the walls are marble, and mirrors and gilding, where there are flowery carpets and Louis Quinze chairs and the true American heat. I think then of the kitchens of Pantyreos and Penyrhaul, as Israel in exile remembered Syon.

But it is not in summertime that it is best to remember these places, excellent though the thought of their coolness and refreshment may be. I like to think of them as set in a framework of late autumn or deep mid-winter. I will be more curious than De Quincey: no mere bitter wind or frost, not even snow will serve my turn, though each of these has its admirable uses.

But let me have a night late in November, let us say. Every leaf has long been down, save that the beech hedgerow in the sheltered forest road will keep its tawny copper all through the winter. Rain has been sweeping along the valleys for days past in giant misty pillars, the brooks are bank high with red, foaming water; down every steep field little hedgerow streams come pouring. In the farmyards the men go about their work clad in sacks, and if they may will shelter under penthouses and find work to do in the barns.

Give me a night in the midst of such weather, and then think of the farm atop the hill, to which two good miles of deep, wandering lane go climbing, and mix the rain with a great wind from the mountain: and then think of entering the place which I have described, set now for the old act of winter. The green shutters are close fastened without the window, the settle is curved about the hearth, and that great cavern is ablaze and glorious with heaped wood and coals, and the white walls golden with the light of the leaping flames. And those within can hear the rain dashing upon shutter and upon closed door, and the fire hisses now and again as stray drops fall down the chimney; and the great wind shakes the trees and goes roaring down the hillside to the valley and moans and mutters about the housetop.

A man will leave his place, snug in shelter, in the deepest glow of the fire, and go out for a moment and open but a little of the door in the porch and see all the world black and wild and wet, and then come back to the light and heat and thank God for his home, wondering whether any are still abroad on such a night of tempest.

Looking back on my native country as I first remember it, I have often regretted that I was not born say twenty or thirty years earlier. I should then have seen more of a singular social process, which I can only call the Passing of the Gentry. In my father's parish this had taken place very long before my day, or his either. Indeed, I am not quite sure that any armigerous families had ever inhabited Llanddewi; though I have a dim notion that certain old farmhouses were pointed out to me as having been "gentlemen's houses." But an adjoining parish had once held three very ancient families of small gentry. One was still in existence well within my recollection, another became extinct in the legitimate line soon after I was born, and the third had been merged in other and larger inheritances.

There were no Perrotts left, and their house had been "restored," and was occupied as a farm. I often sat under their memorials in the little church, and admired their arms, three golden pears, and their crest, a parrot; altogether a pretty example of *heraldia cantans,* or punning heraldry. Of the other two houses one was a pleasant, rambling, moldering place, yellow-washed, verandahed, and on the whole more like a *petit manoir* in Touraine than a country house in England. The third mansion was a sixteenth-century house built in the L shape, and here dwelt in my childhood the last of the ancient gentry of the place.

Even he was descended from the old family in the female line. The old race had been named Meyrick, and they had given land in the thirteenth century that a light might burn before the altar of a neighboring church forever. The family affirmed that at one time they had owned all the land that could be seen from a certain high place near their house, and very possibly

the tradition was a true one. They had remained faithful to the Latin Church through all the troubles — up
to the year of Napoleon Bonaparte's sacring as Em-
peror by the Pope in Notre-Dame. And when the
reigning squire of Lansoar heard the news he raged
with fury, and saying, as the story goes, "Damn such
a Pope as that!" left the Roman Church forever. His
grandson, whom I knew, always read the Bible in the
Douay version and praised the Papists. Indeed, he used
often to end up, addressing my father, "In fact they tell
me that you're more than half a Roman Catholic
yourself, and I like you none the worse for it!"

He was an extraordinary old man. In his youth he
had been busy one morning packing up his portmanteau to go to Oxford. News came that his father was
ruined; it was probably in the wild smash of specula-
tion that brought down Sir Walter Scott. The young
man quietly unpacked his portmanteau and took possession of the mill, not many yards from his own door.
He ground corn for the farmers; he did well; he moved
into Newport, and became, I think, an importer of
Irish butter. Probably, also, he had his share in the
industrial developments of Glamorganshire and Mon-
mouthshire, then at the height of their prosperity. At
any rate in twenty years or so the fortunes of the old
house were redeemed. The drawing room of Lansoar
had been used as a barn for storing corn; in my day it
was the most gracious and grave room that I have ever
seen. The old family portraits were back on the walls,
the old tapestried chairs were in their places, there was
not a thing in the room less than a hundred years old,
and the squire sat beside his hearth, looking — as I have
found out since those days — exactly like Henry IV of
France.

He had traveled a good deal in his time, and was
supposed to have had his fancy taken by the clothes

he had seen worn by the Heidelberg students. So he wore an odd sort of vestment striped with black and dull red, and gathered in with a belt of the same stuff. We called it a blouse, but it must have been something of the shape of a Norfolk jacket. In the evening he would put on a black velvet coat which, as he told me, he got from Poole's at the price of five guineas. Smoking he abominated, and it was never allowed at Lansoar, save when Mr. Williams of Llangibby was a guest.

The owner of Lansoar was in many ways a kindly and benevolent old gentleman, but I think we in the country were chiefly proud of his temper. It was said to be terrific, even in a land of furious, quickly-raised rages. People told how they had seen the old man's white moustache bristling up to his eyes; this was a sign that the fire was kindled. And, as I once heard him say, "the Meyricks always get white with love and hate." It was said that his sister was the only person who met him on something like equal terms. She was an ancient gentlewoman with a tremendous aquiline nose and was more like a marquise of 1793 going proudly to instant execution than can possibly be imagined. She and her brother differed — it is much too mild a word, I am sure — so fiercely as to what were the true armorial bearings of the family that when these were to be emblazoned above the dining room hearth a compromise had to be arranged, and two shields were painted, one on each side.

I am sorry that I was too young to observe Lansoar and its ways with intelligent interest. The people that lived there were of a race and sort that have now perished utterly out of the land; there never will be such people again. But I was banished from Lansoar for the last year or two of the old squire's life. I had left school and was at a loose end at home, and I heard I had fallen under heavy displeasure. It seemed that the descendant of the Meyricks had known a doctor who had lived in Paris on five shillings a week at the beginning of the nineteenth century; he wished to know why I was not living in London on five shillings a week in 1880. The answer would have been that I had neither five shillings nor five pence a week; but one did not answer Mr. James of Lansoar.

I am heartily sorry that the class which he represented has perished. I am sorry to think of all their houses scattered over Gwent; now mere memorials of something that is done forever and ended. One came upon these houses in every other valley, on every other hillside, looking pleasantly towards the setting sun. They are noble old places, even though they are noble in a humble way; there are no Haddon Halls in Gwent. But these old homes of the small gentry of the borderland — now for the most part used as farmhouses — show their lineage in the dignity of their proportions, in the carved armorial bearings of their porches. The pride of race that belonged to the Morgans, Herberts, Meyricks that once lived in them has passed into their stones, and still shines there.

*T*here is a great book that I am hoping to write one of these fine days. I have been hoping to write it, I may say, since 1898, or '99, and somewhere about the latter year I did write as many as a dozen pages. The *magnum opus* so far conducted did not wholly displease me, and yet it was not good enough to urge me forward in the task. And so it has languished ever since then, and I am afraid I have lost the MSS. that contained all that there was of it long ago. Seriously, of course, it would not have been a great book if it had been ever so prosperously continued and ended; but it would have been at least a curious book, and even now I feel conscious of warm desire at the thought of writing it — some day. For the idea of it came to me as follows:

I had been thinking at the old century end of the work that I had done in the fifteen years or so before, and it suddenly dawned upon me that this work, pretty good or pretty bad, or as it may be, had all been the expression of one formula, one endeavor. What I had been doing was this: I had been inventing tales in which and by which I had tried to realize my boyish impressions of that wonderful magic Gwent. Say that I had walked and wandered by unknown roads, and suddenly, after climbing a gentle hill, had seen before me for the first time the valley of the Usk, just above Newbridge. I think it was on one of those strange days of summer when the sky is at once grey and luminous that I achieved this adventure. There are no clouds in the upper air, the sky is simply covered with a veil which is, as I say, both grey and luminous, and there is no breath of wind, and every leaf is still.

But now and again as the day goes on the veil will brighten, and the sun almost appear; and then here and there in the woods it is as if white moons were descending. On such a day, then, I saw that wonderful and most lovely valley; the Usk, here purged of its muddy tidal waters, now like the sky, grey and silvery and luminous, winding in mystic esses, and the dense forest bending down to it, and the grey stone bridge crossing it. Down the valley in the distance was Caer-leon-on-Usk; over the hill, somewhere in the lower slopes of the forest, Caerwent, also a Roman city, was buried in the earth, and gave up now and again strange relics — fragments of the temple of "Nodens, god of the depths." I saw the lonely house between the dark forest and the silver river, and years after I wrote "The Great God Pan," an endeavor to pass on the vague,

indefinable sense of awe and mystery and terror that I
had received.

This, then, was my process: to invent a story which
would recreate those vague impressions of wonder and
awe and mystery that I myself had received from the
form and shape of the land of my boyhood and youth;
and as I thought over this and meditated on the futility
— or comparative futility — of the plot, however ingenious, which did not exist to express emotions of one
kind or another, it struck me that it might be possible
to reverse the process. Could one describe hills and
valleys, woods and rivers, sunrise and sunset, buried
temples and moldering Roman walls so that a story
should be suggested to the reader? Not, of course, a
story of material incidents, not a story with a plot in
the ordinary sense of the term, but an interior tale of
the soul and its emotions; could such a tale be suggested in the way I have indicated? Such is to be the
plan of the "great" book which is not yet written. I
mention it here chiefly because I would lay stress on
my doctrine that in the world of imagination the child
is indeed father of the man, that the man is nothing
more than the child with an improved understanding
certainly, with all sorts of technical advantages in the
way of information and in the arts of expression, but,
on the other hand, with the disadvantages of a dimmed
imaginative eye and a weakened vision. There have
been a few men who have kept the awe and the surmise
of earlier years and have added to those miraculous
gifts the acquired accomplishments of age and instruction; and these are the only men who are entitled to
the name of genius. I have said already that in my
boyhood and youth I was a deep and learned student
of the country about my home, and that I always saw
it as a kind of fairyland. And, cross-examining my
memory, I find that I have in no way exaggerated or

overcolored these early and earliest impressions. Fairyland is too precise a word; I would rather say that I saw
everything in something of the spirit in which the first
explorers gazed on the tropical luxuriance and strangeness of the South American forests, on the rock cities
of Peru, on the unconjectured seas that burst upon
them from that peak in Darien, on the wholly unimagi-
ned splendors of the Mexican monarchy. So it was with
me as a child. I came into a strange country, and
strange it ever remained to me, so that when I left it
forever there were still hills within sight and yet un-
trodden, lanes and paths of which I knew the beginning but not the end. For it is to be understood that
country folk are in this respect like Londoners: that
they have their customary tracks and ways which lead
more or less to some end or other; it is only occasionally that either goes out determined not to find his way
but to lose it, to stray for the very sake of straying. Thus
I walked many times in Wentwood and became familiar with the Roman road that passes for some distance
along the summit of that ancient forest, but only once,
I think, did I set out from the yellow verge of the Severn
and cross the level Moors — a belt of fen country that
might well lie between Ely and Brandon; really, no
doubt "y môr," the sea — and wonder for a while at the
bastioned and battlemented ruins of Caldicot Castle,
and so mount up by the outer hills and woods of the
forest, through Caerwent, past the Foresters' Oaks, a
grove of trees that were almost awful in the magnifi-
cence of their age and their decay, and so climb to the
ridge and look down on the Usk and the more familiar
regions to the west.

And, as you may judge, it was only the knowledge
that one must not frighten one's family out of its wits
and that camping out in forests without food or drink
is highly inconvenient that kept me on this compara-

tively straight path. So all the while, as I paced an unknown way, yet more unknowns were beckoning to me on right and left. Paths full of promise allured me into green depths, the wildest heights urged me to attempt them, cottages in orchard dells seemed so isolated from all the world that they and theirs must be a part of enchantment. And so I crossed Wentwood, and felt not that I knew it, but that it was hardly to be known.

I have already mentioned, I think, that I was an only child. Add to this statement that I had no little cousins available as play-fellows, some of these being domiciled in Anglesea, others in London; that it was only by the merest chance and on the rarest occasions that I ever saw any children at all, and I have given some notion of the extreme solitude of my upbringing. I grew up, therefore, all alone so far as other children were concerned, and though I went to school, school did not seem to make much difference to my habit of mind. I was eleven years old at the time, and I suppose I was "set" to loneliness. I passed the term as a sort of interlude amongst strangers, and came home to my friendly lanes, to my deep and shadowy and secret valleys, as a man returns to his dear ones and his dear native fields after exile amongst aliens and outlanders.

I came back, then, again and again to solitude. There were no children's parties for me, no cricket, no football, and I was heartily glad of it, for I should have abhorred all these diversions with shudderings of body and spirit. My father and mother apart, I loved to be by myself, with unlimited leisure for mooning and loafing and roaming and wandering from lane to lane, from wood to wood. Constantly I seemed to be finding new, hitherto unsuspected tracks, to be emerging from deep lanes and climbing hills so far but seen from the distance, matters of surmise, and now trodden and found to be Darien peaks giving an outlook upon strange worlds of river and forest and bracken-covered slope. Wondering at these things, I never ceased to wonder; and even when I knew a certain path and became familiar with it I never lost my sense of its marvels, as they appeared to me.

I have read curious and perplexed commentaries on that place in Sir Thomas Browne in which he declares his life up to the period of the "Religio Medici" to have been "a miracle of thirty years, which to relate were not a history, but a piece of poetry." Dr. Johnson, summing up the known events of Browne's early life, finds therein nothing in the least miraculous; Southey says the miracle was the great writer's preservation from atheism; Leslie Stephen considers that the strangeness "consists rather in Browne's view of his own history than in any unusual phenomena." "View of his own history" seems a little vague; but however critical sagacity may determine the sense of the passage, I would very willingly adopt it to describe these early years of mine, spent in that rectory amongst the wild hills of Gwent. Of my private opinion, I think there can be little doubt that when Sir Thomas Browne used the word "miraculous" he was thinking not of miracles in the accepted sense as things done contrary to the generally observed laws of nature, but rather of his vision of the world, of his sense of a constant wonder latent in all things. Stevenson, I believe, had some sense of this doctrine as applied to landscape, at least, when he said that there were certain scenes — I forget how he particularized them — which demanded their stories, which cried out, as it were, to have tales indited to fit their singular aspects. This, I think I have shown, is a crude analysis. I should put it thus: this group of pines, this lonely shore, or whatever the scene may be, has made the soul thrill with an emotion intense but vague in the sense in which music is vague; and the man of letters does his best to realize — rather, perhaps, to actualize — this emotion by inventing a tale about the pines or the sands. Such at all events was my state through all the years of boyhood and of youth: everything to me was wonderful, everything visible was the veil of an invisible secret. Before an oddly shaped stone I was ready to fall into a sort of reverie or meditation, as if it had been a fragment of paradise or fairyland. There was a certain herb of the fields that grew plentifully in Gwent, that even now I cannot regard without a kind of reverence; it bears a spire of small yellow blossoms, and its leaves when crushed give out a very pungent, aromatic odor. This odor was to me a separate revelation or mystery, as if no one in the world had smelt it but myself, and I ceased not to admire even when a countryman told me that it was good for stone, if you gathered it "under the planet Juniper."

And here, may I say in passing, that in my opinion the country parson, with all the black-coated class, knows next to nothing of the true minds of the country folk. I feel certain that my father, if asked by a Royal Commission or some such valuable body, "What influence has astrology on your parishioners?" would have answered: "They have never heard of such a thing." In later years I have wondered as to the possible fields which extended beyond the bounds of our ignorance. I have wondered, for example, whether, by any possibility, there were waxen men, with pins in them, hidden in very secret nooks in any of the Llanddewi cottages.

But this is a mere side-issue. To return to my topic, to that attitude of the child-mind which almost says in its heart, "things are because they are wonderful," I am reminded of one of the secret societies with which I have had the pleasure of being connected. This particular society issued a little MS. volume of instructions to those who were to be initiated, and amongst these instructions was the note: "remember that nothing exists which is not God." "How can I possibly realize that?" I said to one of the members of the society. "When I read it I was looking at the tiles on each side of my fireplace in Gray's Inn, and they are of the beastliest design it is possible to imagine. I really cannot see anything of Divinity in those tiles." I do not remember how my objection was met; I don't think it was met. But, looking back, I believe that, as a child, I realized something of the spirit of the mystic injunction. Everywhere, through the darkness and the mists of the childish understanding, and yet by the light of the child's illumination, I saw *latens deitas*; the whole earth, down to the very pebbles, was but the veil of a quickening and adorable mystery. Hazlitt said that the man of genius spent his whole life in telling the world what he had known himself when he was eighteen. Waiving utterly — I am sorry to say — the title of man of genius, I would reaffirm Hazlitt's proposition on lower grounds. I would say that he who has any traffic with the affairs of the imagination has found out all the wisdom that he will ever know, in this life at all events, by the age of eighteen or thereabouts. And it is probable that Hazlitt, though he never dreamed of it, was but re-expressing those sentences in the Holy Gospels which deal with the intimate relationship between children and "the Kingdom of Heaven." In the popular conception, of course, both amongst priests and people, these texts are understood to refer to the innocence of childhood. But a little reflection will satisfy anyone that in the true sense of the word children are only innocent as a stone is innocent, as a stick is innocent; that is, they are incapable of committing the special offences which to our modern and utterly degraded system of popular ethics constitute the whole matter of morality and immorality. I remember a few years ago reading how an illustrious Primitive Methodist testified on the sacred mount of Primitive Methodism at some anniversary of the society. He said that his old grandmother had implored him when he was a boy never to drink, never to gamble, never to break the Sabbath, and, he concluded triumphantly, "I have never done any of these things."

"Therefore I am a good Christian" is the conclusion evidently suggested. This poor man, it may be said, knew no better, but I am much mistaken if the majority of our Anglican clergy would not accept his statement as a good confession of the faith. The New Testament for all these people has been written in vain; they will still believe that a good Christian is one who drinks a cup of cocoa at 9.30 and is in bed by ten sharp. And to such persons, of course, the texts which assert the necessity of becoming like little children if we would enter the Kingdom of Heaven are clear enough; it is a mere matter of early hours and plenty of cocoa – or, perhaps, of warm bread and milk. But, personally, I cannot at all symbolize with them. I look back to the time when the mountain and the tiny shining stone, the flower, and the brook were all alike signs and evidences of an ineffable mystery and beauty. I see myself all alone in the valley, under hanging woods, of a still summer evening, entranced, wondering what the secret was that was here almost told, and then, I am persuaded, I came near to the spirit of St. Thomas Aquinas: *Adoro te devote latens Deitas.*

*T*here comes to me from very long ago the memory of a burning afternoon in the hot heart of July. I am not sure whether it was in the dry summer. This was in '68 or '69 — I am not certain which — and it was notable for many things in my recollection. Firstly, the mountain caught fire. This sounds a terrific and unlikely statement, considered with relation to the temperate and reasonable geology of this land, which has known nothing for many æons of volcanoes or burning mountains. What had happened, of course, was that the heather and wild growth on the mountain had somehow been fired, and so all through that hot August I remember looking westward to the great mountain wall, and watching the dun fume that drifted along its highest places; looking with a certain dread, for there was something apocalyptic in the sight.

Another notable event was the failure of the water supply. The rectory stood almost on top of a long hill that mounted up from the valley of the Soar, there were no ponds or tanks in its curtilage and the drought of this year exhausted the water in the great butt that stood in the yard and received the streams from the roof in rainy weather. This, of course, was not drinking water; that we obtained always from a well deep in the brake, about a quarter of a mile from the house; and without contempt for other and more elaborate beverages, I may say that there are few drafts more delicious than cold well-water, dripping from the rock, and shaded in its hollow basin by the overhanging trees. Our London water is, I believe, perfectly wholesome, but it is absolutely tasteless, no doubt through the manifold purifications and purgations which it has undergone. But well-water has a savor and a character of its own, and the product of one well will often differ in a very marked degree from that of another. Before

my day, oddly enough, we had in the county a con-
noisseur or gourmet of wells. He was a clergyman, and
he had been heard to boast that he had tasted the water
of every well in the forest of Wentwood. Our own well
in the rectory brake was thought excellently of by good
judges of clear cold water.

I think it was in this year of the burning mountain
that the rectory paid a call on Mr. and Mrs. Roger
Gibbon, of the Wern, on a blazing afternoon. They
were very old people, and the stock of the Gibbons —
I am not using their real name — was one of the most
ancient and honored in the land of Gwent. I suppose,
indeed, that they would look on many dukes as parve-
nus of yesterday. Furthermore, this branch of the race
was quite comfortable and well-to-do in money matters.

They received my father and my mother and myself
with the heartiest kindness — they had known my
father from his boyhood — and insisted on the necessity of some refreshment. So presently the maid came
in with a tray and old Roger solemnly mixed for my
father and mother, for his wife and himself, four
reeking glasses of hot gin. I think that, all things
considered, this was the very strangest refreshment ever
offered. The old people swallowed their boiling spirit
with relish, my parents took their dose with shuddering
politeness, and the thermometer rose steadily. Roger
and Caroline had been quarreling about a carpet before
we came, and after a decent interval the quarrel was
resumed. Roger addressed himself to my mother.

"She would buy it too small. I told her it would be
too small, and there it is, with three or four feet of the
floor showing. And what do you think she says, Mrs.
Machen? She says she will have the bare boards painted
green to match the carpet. I say that's ridiculous, don't
you think so? [Without waiting for an answer, and

bellowing to deaf old Caroline.] There, Caroline, I told you what everyone would say. Mrs. Machen says it's ridiculous. The idea of painting the boards green!"

And the old man, turning to my father, told him in a lower voice and with considerable enjoyment of some home-made wine that his wife had concocted. She had stored it in a cupboard in their bedroom, and Roger told how he used to lie awake at night laughing as he listened to the bottles bursting, the old lady being much too deaf to hear the reports.

Old Gibbon was an expert shot, but he could never be persuaded to use the new-fangled percussion caps. He brought down his birds to the last by means of flint and steel. He was an enthusiastic fox hunter also, but he never hunted on horseback. Up to something past the middle of his life the Llangibby Hounds had been hunted afoot, the Rector of Llangibby being the master, and afoot Roger Gibbon followed them up to his old age. And so cunning had he become in matter of wind and scent and lie of the country that he rarely failed to be in at the death. I doubt whether he knew much of the world outside of a twenty-mile radius, Caerleon being taken as the center of the circle. But when Roger Gibbon was quite an old man people told him that he ought to see London. So he went to London. He walked out of Paddington Station and saw London, as he thought; and, filled with a great horror and disgust and terror at what he had seen, he trotted back into the station, and paced the platform till the next train for the west started. He got into that train, and returned to the Wern and to the shelter and companionship of his hills and woods, and there abode till the ending of his long days.

It was strange how in those times people were fixed in the soil, so that for many miles round everybody knew everybody, or at least knew of everybody. It is all over, I suppose, and again I think it is a pity that it is over. It was a part of the old life of the friendly fires, and the friendly faces, and when, rarely enough, in this great desert of London, I meet a friend of those old days, I think we both feel as if we were surviving tribesmen of some sept that has been "literally annihilated" or "almost decimated" — to use our modern English.

One says: "Do you remember that walk over Mynydd Fawr to the Holy Well?" The other replies: "How good the beer at the Three Salmons tasted that day we walked all the way from Caerleon on the Old Usk Road." "Let me see; when was that?" "April, '83." And we look on one another and, lo, our heads have whitened and our eyes are beginning to grow dim.

But, as an instance of the fellowship and brotherhood that there was in the land of Gwent in the old days, here is a true story. I have told of fierce old Mr. James, of Lansoar, the ancient squire. Well, there had been a raging and tremendous quarrel between Mr. James and a neighboring farmer called Williams, and as Williams was an honest and excellent and placable old man, there was not much doubt as to who was the aggressor. After years of hate, on one side at all events, a false rumor went about the county that Mr. James had lost all his money, in "Turkish Bonds," I think. Then did old Mr. Williams, the farmer, go up one night secretly to old Mr. James, the squire, and altogether heedless of the white face and the furious glance and the bristling moustache that greeted him, he offered all he had to his enemy.

May he remember me from his happy place.

Chapter II

*B*y this time I hope that I have made a sort of picture of my conditions as they were up to the time that I left school at the age of seventeen. Solitude and woods and deep lanes and wonder; these were the chief elements of my life. One thing, however, I have so far omitted, that is the matter of books, which I will now consider.

And, firstly, I must record with deep thankfulness the circumstance that as soon as I could read I had the run of a thoroughly ill-selected library; or, rather, of a library that had not been selected at all. My father's collection, if that serious word may be applied to a hugger-mugger of books, had grown up anyhow and nohow, and in it the most revered stocks had mingled with the most frivolous. There were the Fathers, in the English version made by the Tractarians, and there was also no end of "yellowbacks" bought at Smith's book-stalls on railway journeys. There was a row of little Elzevir classics, "with the Sphere," bound in parchment that had grown golden with its two hundred and odd years; there was also Mr. Verdant Green in his tattered paper wrapper as my father had bought him at Oxford. Next to Verdant Green you might very likely find the Dialogues of Erasmus in seventeenth-century leather, and Borrow in his original boards — we read Borrow at Llanddewi long before there were any Borrovians — might hide an odd volume of "Martin Chuzzlewit" (in a "Railway Edition") which had tumbled to the back of the shelf. Hard by stood Copleston's "Prælectiones Academicæ," and close to it a complete set of Brontë books, including Mrs. Gaskell's "Life," all these in yellowish linen covers, being, I imagine, the first one-volume edition issued by the publishers. And here again Llanddewi in the woods may claim to have been in advance of its age, for we were devoted to the name of Brontë.

Suppose the weather did not beckon me, I would begin to go about the house on the search of books. I might have "Wuthering Heights" in my mind and be chasing that amazing volume very closely, and be, in fact, hot on the scent, when I would be brought up sharply by my grandfather's Hebrew grammar. I always loved the shape and show of the Hebrew character, and have meant to learn the language from 1877 onwards, but have not yet thoroughly mastered the alphabet. I once, indeed, got so advanced as to be able to spell out the Yiddish posters which cover the walls in the East End of London, and I remember being much amused when I had deciphered a most mystic, reverend-looking word and found that it read "Bishopsgyte." But I believe that in Yiddish the two "yods" represent the "a" sound.

Well, this Hebrew grammar would distract me from the hunt of Emily Brontë's masterpiece, and by the time I had decided that Monday would be soon enough for a serious beginning in Hebrew, while I meditated in the meanwhile on the beauty of the names of the four classes of accents — Emperors, Kings, Princes, and Dukes, I think — it was likely enough that I had got hold of Alison's "History of Europe," or "The

Bible in Spain," or a book on Brasses. And by the time
I had gloated over the horrors of the French Revolu-
tion as described in Alison, or had marveled at Borrow
in the character of a Protestant colporteur, or had
admired the pictured brasses of Sir Robert de Septvans,
Sir Roger de Trumpington — winnowing fans on the
coat-armor of the one, trumpets on the shield of the
other — and Abbot Delamere of St. Albans it was
teatime, and I probably spent the rest of the evening
with a bound volume of "Chambers's Journal," "All
the Year Round," "Cornhill," or "The Welcome Guest."
These were always a great resource; and I particularly
wish that I still possessed "The Welcome Guest," a
popular weekly dating from the late 'fifties of last
century. It was full of work by people who afterwards
became famous, and now, again, are fading into for-
getfulness. John Hollingshead we still remember,
though it is only the elderly who can tell much now
of "the sacred lamp of burlesque," which was kept
burning at the Gaiety. Hollingshead was a contributor
to "The Welcome Guest," so also were the Brothers
Mayhew and the Brothers Brough, so on a great scale
was George Augustus Sala, who wrote in it "Twice
Round the Clock" and something that was called, I
fancy, "Make Your Game or, the Adventures of the
Stout Gentleman, the Thin Gentleman, and the Man
with the Iron Chest." This was a "lively" account of a
visit to the gaming tables then existing in Germany.
The Stout Gentleman was one of the Mayhews, the
Man with the Iron Chest was Sala himself; and I met
the Thin Gentleman many years afterwards in a cock-
loft in Catherine Street, where I was cataloguing books
on magic and alchemy and the secret arts in general.
The cock-loft was over the Vizetellys' publishing office,
and the Thin Gentleman was old Mr. Vizetelly. We
"larned" him to publish a translation of "La Terre" by

sending him, an old man past seventy, to jail for three months. He died soon afterwards; I forget whether his death took place before or after the very handsome and official and "respectable" reception and entertainment that were given to Zola on his visiting England.

I must say that I should like to see the old "Welcome Guest" volume again. I am afraid I should not admire its literature very much, for Sala, the chief contributor, had already acquired those vicious mannerisms which pleased the injudicious. He would speak of Billingsgate as a "piscatorial bourse," for instance. I am afraid I should find it all terribly old-fashioned. But I should like to hold the fat volume again and glance through its pages, for they would bring back to me the long winter evenings, and the rectory fire burning cheerfully, and the heavy red curtains drawn close over the windows, shutting out the night.

I must say that I found a great joy and resource in these old magazines. If one were in a mood averse from reading in the solid block, if the hour did not seem propitious for beginning once more "Pickwick" from the beginning, it was a delight to think of those bound volumes all in a row, and of the inexhaustible supply of mixed literature which they contained. For just as there was always the chance, and indeed the likelihood, of making new discoveries in the happy confusion of the Llanddewi library, so it was with these rows of "Household Words," "Chambers's," "All the Year Round," "Welcome Guest," and "Cornhill"; there was always the possibility of a find; some tale or essay hitherto overlooked or neglected might turn out to be full of matter and entertainment. And so the most unlikely events happened. You would expect to find good things of all sorts in a magazine edited by Charles Dickens, but you would hardly expect to find there the curious thing or the out-of-the-way thing. Still, it was in a volume of "Household Words" that I first read about alchemy in a short series of papers which (I have since recognized) were singularly well-informed and enlightened. I do not wish it to be understood that I myself have any strong convictions on the matter of turning inferior metals into superior, though I believe the later trend of science is certainly in favor of the theoretical possibility of such a process. Nor do I hold any distinct brief for the very fascinating doctrine which maintains, or would like to maintain, that the great alchemical books are really symbolical books; that while seeming to relate to lead and gold, to mercury and silver, they hide under these figures intimations as to a profound and ineffable transmutation of the spirit; that the experiment to which they relate is the Great Experiment of the mystics, which is the experiment of God. This, I say, is a fascinating theory; whether it have any truth in it I know not, and perhaps it is one of those questions of which Sir Thomas Browne speaks; questions difficult, indeed, and perplexed, but not beyond all conjecture. But, however this may be, I recollect that those articles in that old, half-calf bound volume of "Household Words," while not affirming this, that, or the other doctrine as to alchemy in so many distinct words, did suggest that a few of the old alchemists, at all events, were something more than blundering simpletons engaged on a quest which was a patent absurdity, which could only have been entertained by the besotted superstition of "the dark ages," which had this one claim to our attention inasmuch as the modern science of chemistry rose from the ashes of its foolish fires.

This is not the place for a discussion of the art of Thrice Great Hermes; the matter is cited here as an example of the odd and unexpected way in which my attention, I being some eight or nine years old, was directed to a singular and perplexing subject which has engaged my curiosity at intervals ever since. I see myself sitting on a stool by the rectory hearth, propping up "Household Words" against the fender, quite ravished by the story of Nicholas Flamel, who found by chance "The Book of Abraham the Jew," who journeyed all over Europe in search of one who would interpret its figures to him, who succeeded at last in the Operation of the Great Work, and was discovered by the King's Chamberlain living in great simplicity, eating cabbage soup with Pernelle, his wife. These fireside studies of mine must have been made forty-three or forty-four years ago, but I still think the story of Nicholas Flamel and Pernelle, his wife, an enchanting one. But then I re-read the tale of Aladdin and the Wonderful Lamp only the other day, and I am still thrilled and perplexed by that most singular and important fact; that the genie declared himself to be the servant of the Roc's Egg.

I am sorry to have to confess that the rectory shelves held no copy of "The Arabian Nights." I made up this deficiency soon after I went to school by buying an excellent edition, issued, I think, by Routledge for a shilling. This edition is now, the booksellers tell me, out of print, and it is a pity, for now if you want the book there is nothing between an edition obviously meant for the nursery, with gaudy plates, and Lane's version for thirty shillings. I speak not of Burton, for I found myself unable to read a couple of pages of his detestable English, made more terrible by the imitations of the rhymed prose of the original. I came upon something which went very much as follows: —

Then followed the dawn of day, and the Princess
finished her allotted say,

Praise be to the Lord of Light alway, who faileth not
    to send the appointed ray —

and so on, at much greater length; highly ingenious,
no doubt, and also infinitely foolish.

    I remember once wasting hours — nay, days — in the
effort to render Rabelais' "Verses written over the Great
Gate of the Abbey of Thelème" into English, following
as far as I could the rhyme system. Now, according to
the French notion, "don" is a perfect rhyme to "pardon," and so Rabelais wrote: —

Or donné par don,
Ordonne pardon
A cil qui le donne;
Et bien guerdonne
Tout mortel preudhom
Or donné par don.

    That is, the final sound of each line is almost iden-
tical with the final sound of every other line; and of
this I made: —

For given relief,
Forgiven and lief
The giver believe;
And all men that live
May gain the palm leaf
For given relief.

    Soon afterwards, while I was resting from this mighty
effort, I read in Disraeli's "Curiosities of Literature" a
quotation from Martial: Turpe est difficiles habere
nugas — 'Tis folly to sweat o'er a difficult trifle.' I was
convinced of my sin. I suppose that the real translator
when confronted by such puzzles contrives to think of

an indirect rather than a direct solution. For example, the right way of getting the effect of the Arabic jingle into English might be sought by the path of alliteration; or possibly blank verse might give to the English reader something of the same kind of pleasure as that enjoyed by the Oriental in reading a prose which infringes on the region of poetry. And it may be that the queer music of Rabelais could be echoed, at least, in English by the use of assonance.

Here is, indeed, a diversion, but it has arisen, legitimately enough, from that shilling, paper wrapper volume of "The Arabian Nights" bought in 1875 or '76 or thereabouts. And another event of like importance was my seeing De Quincey's "Confessions of an English Opium Eater" at Pontypool Road Station. This also I instantly bought and as instantly loved, and still love very heartily. It always vexes me to detect, as I constantly do detect in modern critics, the subtle desire to run down De Quincey. The critic is afraid to make a frontal attack — the stress of these times will win pardon for the phrase — since he knows that he will be opposed by such splendors and such terrors — "an army with banners" — as the English language can scarce show elsewhere. He is quite aware, since he is, ex hypothesi, an able critic, that De Quincey deliberately used our tongue as if it had been a mighty organ in mightier cathedral, so that the very stones and the far-lifted vault and the hollow spaces of the towers re-echo and reverberate and thrill with tremendous fugal harmonies. And our critics are advised also that De Quincey was no mere player of clever tricks with the language; his was not the amusing Stevensonian method of counting the "l's" and estimating the value of medial "s's" and the terrifying effect of the final reiterated "r." There was none of this; he wrote in the great manner because he thought in the great manner.

The critic cannot deny this; he must admit the beauty and pathos of the Ann episode and of the vision of Jerusalem; but still he will hint a fault and hesitate his dislike of this greater master. The reason is not far to seek. All realism is unpopular, and De Quincey was eminently a realist.

Now I know that I am touching here on a great question. I hope to debate it at length later on; for the moment I would merely say that I define realism as the depicting of eternal, inner realities — the "things that really are" of Plato — as opposed to the description of transitory, external surfaces; the delusory masks and dominoes with which the human heart drapes and hides itself. But, all this apart, I cannot help dwelling on the manner in which I associate these early literary discoveries of mine with the places where they were made.

You may hear friends and lovers discussing after many years the manner of their first meeting; Daphnis as Darby will remind Chloe — now Joan — how they saw one another for the first time at the Smiths' garden-party, and one plate of their bread and butter tasted slightly of onions, and the curate achieved six faults running at lawn-tennis, and it came on to rain. So I can never take up De Quincey without thinking of the dismal platform at Pontypool Road, and the joy of coming home for the holidays, and the mountains all about me as I stood and waited for my father and the trap and read the first pages of the magic book. Those great mountains, and the drive home by the green arched lanes, abounding in flowers, and the very dear look of home amidst its orchards; all these are part and parcel of my joy in the "Confessions" forever. And so again with another noble book; with one of the noblest of all books, as I have ever esteemed it. I am a very small boy; about seven or eight years old, I conceive, and my mother takes me with her to pay a call on Mrs. Gwyn, of Llanfrechfa Rectory. The ladies talk, and I, seeking quietly for something to entertain me, light in a low bookcase on a fat, dumpy little book. I suspect it was the oddity of the shape, the extreme squabness of the volume, that first took my fancy, and then I open the pages — and I have never really closed them. For the dumpy book was a translation of "The Ingenious Gentleman, Don Quixote de la Mancha"; and those are words that will thrill a lettered man as the opening notes of certain fugues of Bach will thrill a musician. I heard nothing of the amiable talk of the ladies. I was deep in the small print — alas! it would now blind my tired eyes — and when my mother rose to go I clung so desperately and piteously to the fat little book that the kind Mrs. Gwyn said she would lend it to me, and I might take it home. For which benevolence I am ever bound to pray for her good estate, or for her soul; as it may chance to be.

So, as Hereford Station spells for me, principally, "The Arabian Nights," as De Quincey is linked with domed mountains and green lanes and the return home: the Ingenious Gentleman advanced to greet me, mysteriously enough, in the drawing room of the rectory of Llanfrechfa, and I shall always reckon Frechfa — the "freckled" — as among the most venerated of the Celtic saints.

*F*or a long time, as it seems to me, I have been talking of discoveries of books; discoveries in our own Llanddewi shelves, in the shelves of neighbors, on railway bookstalls. We shall hear more of books by and by, of books found in very different places — Clare Market and the Strand of 1880 and back streets by Notting

Hill Gate are even now looming before us — so for the present we may hear more of the conditions of that Gwent where I was a boy and a young man.

I have said that I was born just a little too late to witness the Passing of the Gentry. Few of them survived into my day, and I was too young to see with intelligence that which still remained to be seen of the old order. But one thing I do remember, that the gentry of those times, even when they were wealthy, lived with a simplicity that would astonish the people of today. Those who know "Martin Chuzzlewit" will remember how Tigg Montague, who was Montague Tigg, lunched luxuriously in the board room of his city office. The meal was brought in on a tray and consisted of "a pair of cold roast fowls, flanked by some potted meats and a cool salad." There was a bottle of champagne and a bottle of Madeira. This was the luncheon of vulgar and ostentatious luxury in the 'forties; compare it with the kind of midday meal that the modern Montague would eat at the Hôtel Splendide or the Hôtel Glorieux; the meal of the man who eats and drinks as much to impress others with his wealth as to gratify his own appetite.

Well, I have often seen "the old Lord Tredegar" eating his luncheon. My father and I would be in the coffee-room of the King's Head, Newport, waiting for the ostler to put in the pony. And there in one of the boxes sat the old lord — a very wealthy man — eating his luncheon; which was bread and cheese and a tankard of ale. And, oddly enough, on the one occasion on which I visited the Ham, the magnate thereof, Mr. Iltyd Nicholl, was enjoying a meal similar in every respect to that of Lord Tredegar — though I believe he had a little cold apple tart after his cheese. We, of the middle people, always dined at one on meat, pudding, and cheese; tea followed at five, an affair of bread and butter and jam, with, possibly, a caraway loaf. Hot buttered toast was distinctly festal. The day closed so far as meals were concerned with bread and cheese and beer at nine o'clock. On rare occasions, once in three years or so, a number of clergy who called themselves collectively the Ruridecanal Chapter came to hear a paper read and also to a dinner. This would probably consist of a salmon of Severn or Usk — which muddy waters breed incomparably the finest salmon in the world — of a saddle of Welsh mutton from the mountains, and of a rich sweet called, very lightly and unworthily, a trifle. There would be a dessert of almonds and raisins and, according to the season, home-grown apples and pears or greengages. These delicates would be displayed on a service which showed green vine-leaves in relief against a buff ground, bordered with deep purple and gold. It was hideous, and, I should think, Spode.

In the autumn my mother used to concoct a singular dish which she called fermety. It is more generally known as frumenty; you will find it mentioned in Washington Irving's "Christmas," where the squire makes his supper off it on Christmas Eve — no doubt because it was the traditional fasting dish for the Vigil of the Nativity. It was made, so far as I can remember, of the new wheat of the year, of milk, of eggs, of currants, of raisins, of sugar, and of spices, "all working up together in one delicious gravy." No doubt a very honorable dish and a most ancient and Christian pottage; but I am not quite sure that I should like it, if it were proffered to me now. Among the farmers a few of the elder people still breakfasted on *cawl,* a broth made of fat bacon and vegetables, and decorated, oddly enough, with marigold blossoms. And a fine old man whom I once met in a lane spoke violently against tea, as a corrupting thing and a very vain novelty. For women, he said, it might serve, but the breakfast for a man was a quart of cider with a toast. But most of the farming people breakfasted on rashers of bacon, cooked by being hung on hooks before the fire in a Dutch oven. With the bacon they ate potatoes, which were done in a very savory manner. Take cold boiled potatoes, break into small pieces, fry (or rather, *faites sauter*) in bacon fat, then press into a shallow dish, pat to a smooth surface, and brown before the fire. This is a breakfast that goes very well with a keen mountain breath of a morning.

And I believe that cheese always formed part of the farmers' breakfast, as a kind of second or cold course. This was of their own making, and was of the kind called after Caerphilly, a little town with a huge ruinous castle in a hollow of giant hills. It is a white cheese of a creamy consistency and delicate flavor, and is to be commended for the making of Welsh rarebit. The farmers, as I say, ate it at breakfast, again at twelve o'clock dinner, after hot boiled fat bacon and beans or cabbage, and again at tea, where, to their tastes, it seemed to go very well with bread and butter — I find it hard to realize in London that bread and butter can be a choice delicacy — and a sweet, such as an open-work raspberry tart. And, of course, the Caerphilly cheese appeared again at supper, and with bread and onions it was always the hedgerow snack of the man in the fields.

And the cider of that land was good. It was a greenish yellow in color, with a glint of gold in it if held up to the light, as it were a remembrance of the August and September suns that had shone mellow on the deep orchards of Gwent. It was of full body and flavor and strength, smooth on the palate, neither sweet nor sharp; and I do not think there was anyone in Llanddewi parish so poor as not to have a barrel or two in his cellar against Christmastide and snowy nights, though to be sure in years wherein apples were a scanty crop some of the smaller folk increased the bulk of their cider by strange expedients. Pears went to the mill always, and as a matter of course. In most of the orchards there were one or two big pear trees, and possibly the wisdom of the Gwentian ancients had concluded that a slight admixture of pears with the apples improved and mellowed the cider. But in scanty years, when the man with but a few trees saw bare boughs in autumn, he went to his garden, dug up a barrow load or two of parsnips and added them to his apples. I cannot say anything as to the resultant juice, since I never tasted it.

There was no wretched poverty in Llanddewi, because almost everybody had a little land of his own. Tenant farmers there were, of course, who held of Mr. John Hanbury, of Pontypool Park, lord of the manor of Edlogan; a manor named after a certain Edlogion who was a prince of the sixth century and the protector of Cybi Sant. But besides his tenants and those of other landlords there was a numerous race of small freeholders, who owned eighty, fifty, ten acres of land, and so down till you came to a holding of a house and a garden and a mere patch by the roadside. But with a garden and a patch of land a clever cottager of the old school could do a great deal. I remember an old man named Timothy who lived in a house very small and very ancient in the midst of the fields, far, even, from a by-road; and he thought in greengages as a Stock Exchange man thinks in shares. For about his old cottage there were three or four, or maybe half a dozen, greengage trees that had been planted so long ago that they had grown almost to the dignity of timber, and spread wild branches high and low and far and wide, so that one might say that old Timothy lived in a grove or wood of greengage trees. So you may conceive how deeply the poor old man thought of these gages, beside which his little orchard of damsons and bullaces was of small account. A really plentiful crop, when the big boughs were heavy and drooping with rich green, sun-speckled fruit, meant to him abundance and luxury; and bare trees spelt on the other hand a bare winter and some pinching of poverty, though nothing be-yond endurance. Timothy was a smallholder on the smallest scale, but there were many people of two, six, or twelve acres who did very well in their humble way — which I have always thought is the happy way, if one can attain to it. The man would work for a farmer in the day-time, and often be sturdy enough to do many things on his own estate on summer evenings; and all the day long his wife was busy with her pigs and bees and fowls, and perhaps with two or three cows. There was a good market for their produce at Pontypool, a town on the verge of the industrial district, for the colliers and the tinplate workers love to feed richly. I once saw a woman putting the last touches to a flat apple tart in a little tavern called Castell-y-bwch (Bucks' Castle) on the mountain side. She drew out the tart from the oven, prised open the lid of pastry, and inserted some half-pound of butter and half pound of moist Demerara sugar, and then put back the lid and replaced the pastry in the oven; so that apple juice, sugar, butter should fuse all together. That is a fair sample of hill cookery; other people of the hills would buy fresh butter at a high price, and give what they were asked for "green" Caerphilly cheese, still melting from the press; and they loved to plaster butter heavily on hot new bread and then crown all with an equal depth of golden honey. And they had a goodly appetite also for great fat salmon, caught in the yellow Usk water; and so the fishermen of Caerleon and the little farmers of such parishes as Llanddewi profited hugely by these mountain tastes.

Many years afterwards I lived for a short while on the Chiltern Hills. Here was a different tale. In a whole parish there was, I think, barely a single small holder; the little properties had all been bought up by the great landlords. There was no comfort about the tumble-down, leaky cottages which, in many cases, depended for their drinking water supply on dirty water-butts. None of the farm laborers had fowls or pigs or bees; the farmers, their employers, did not allow the men to keep pigs or fowls lest they should be tempted to steal corn and meal.

So the poorer folk were divided into two classes — the good-humored wastrels, who "went on the parish" at the slightest provocation and without the slightest shame, and a few more prosperous, sour, ill-mannered boors, who were consumed with an acrid "Liberalism" and with a rancorous envy of anyone better off than themselves.

But at Llanddewi the small holder of land, so far from envying or hating the great landlord, took, as it were, a pride in him. I remember Mrs. Owen Tudor, owner of nine or ten rough acres of wild land in Llanddewi, being both grieved and angry when she heard that a great and ancient Gwentian house might be forced to sell a certain portion of their estates through the pressure of bad times in the early 'eighties. She, too, was a landowner — of rushes chiefly and alder copses and bracken — and of ancient, though unbla-zoned, family, and if the great Morgans suffered, so also did she suffer.

*I*t comes to my mind that I must by no means forget Sir Walter Scott and all that he did for me. And to get at him it is necessary that we enter the drawing room at Llanddewi. I was amused the other day to see in an old curiosity shop near Lincoln's Inn Fields amongst the rarities displayed small china jars or pots with a picture of two salmon against a background of leafage on the lid. I remember eating potted salmon out of just such jars as these, and now even in my lifetime they appear to have become curious. So, perhaps, if I describe a room which was furnished in 1864 that also may be found to be curious. I may note, by the way, that we always applied the word "parlor" — which properly means drawing room, and is still, I think, used in that sense in the United States of America — to the dining room, which was also our living room for general, everyday use. So Sir Walter Scott speaks of a "dining-parlor," and Mr. Pecksniff, entering Todgers's, of the "eating-parlor." And now the word only occurs in public-houses, in the phrase "parlor prices," and even that use is becoming obsolete.

But as for the Llanddewi drawing room: the walls were covered with a white paper, on which was repeated at regular intervals a diamond-shaped design in pale, yellowish buff. The carpet was also white; on it, also at regular intervals, were bunches of very red roses and very green leaves. In the exact center of the room was a round rosewood table standing on one leg, and consequently shaky. This was covered with a vivid green cloth, trimmed with a bright yellow border. In the center of the cloth was a round mat, apparently made of scarlet and white tags or lengths of wool; this supported the lamp of state. It was of white china and of alabastrous appearance, and it burned colza oil. One had to wind it up at intervals as if it had been a clock.

In the sitting room, before the coming of paraffin, we usually burned "composite" candles; two when we were by ourselves, four when there was company.

Over the drawing room mantelpiece stood a large, high mirror in a florid gilt frame. Before it were two vases of cut-glass, with alternate facets of dull white and opaque green, of a green so evil and so bilious and so hideous that I marvel how the human mind can have conceived it. And yet my heart aches, too, when, as rarely happens, I see in rubbish shops in London back streets vases of like design and color. Somewhere in the room was a smaller vase of Bohemian glass; its designs in "ground" glass against translucent ruby. This vase, I think, must have stood on the whatnot, a triangular pyramidal piece of furniture that occupied one corner and consisted of shelves getting smaller and smaller as they got higher.

Against one wall stood a cabinet, of inlaid wood, velvet lined, with glass doors. On the shelves were kept certain pieces of Nantgarw china, some old wine-glasses with high stems, and a collection of silver shoe-buckles and knee-buckles, and two stoneware jugs. The pictures — white mounts and gilt frames — were watercolors and chromo-lithographs. Against one of the windowpanes hung a painting on glass, depicting a bouquet of flowers in an alabaster jar. There was a plaster cast in a round black frame, which I connect in my mind with the Crystal Palace and the Prince Consort, and an "Art Union," whatever that may be: it displayed a very fat little girl curled up apparently amidst wheat sheaves. A long stool in bead-work stood on the hearthrug before the fire; and a fire-screen, also in bead work, shaped like a banner, was suspended on a brass stand. On a bracket in one corner was the marble bust of Lesbia and her Sparrow; beneath it in a hanging bookcase the Waverley Novels, a brown row of golden books.

I can see myself now curled up in all odd corners of the rectory reading "Waverley," "Ivanhoe," "Rob Roy," "Guy Mannering," "Old Mortality," and the rest of them, curled up and entranced so that I was deaf and gave no answer when they called to me, and had to be roused to life — which meant tea — with a loud and repeated summons. But what can they say who have been in fairyland? Notoriously, it is impossible to give any true report of its ineffable marvels and delights. Happiness, said De Quincey, on his discovery of the paradise that he thought he had found in opium, could be sent down by the mail-coach; more truly I could announce my discovery that delight could be contained in small octavos and small type, in a bookshelf three feet long. I took Sir Walter to my heart with great joy, and roamed, enraptured, through his library of adventures and marvels as I roamed through the lanes and hollows, continually confronted by new enchantments and fresh pleasures. Perhaps I remember most acutely my first reading of "The Heart of Midlothian," and this for a good but external reason. I was suffering from the toothache of my life while I was reading it; from a toothache that lasted for a week and left me in a sort of low fever — as we called it then. And I remember very well as I sat, wretched and yet rapturous, by the fire, with a warm shawl about my face, my father saying with a grim chuckle that I would never forget my first reading of "The Heart of Midlothian." I never have forgotten it, and I have never forgotten that Sir Walter Scott's tales, with every deduction for their numerous and sometimes glaring faults, have the root of the matter in them. They are vital literature, they are of the heart of true romance. What is vital literature, what is true romance? Those are difficult questions which I once tried to answer, according to my lights, in a book called "Hieroglyphics"; here I will merely say that vital literature is something as remote as you can possibly imagine from the short stories of the late Guy de Maupassant.

The hanging bookcase in the drawing room under the marble bust of Lesbia and her Sparrow is not only rich and golden in my memory from its being the habitation of the Waverley Novels. This had been treasure enough, indeed, to make the shelves forever dear; but there was more than this. The bookcase held, besides Sir Walter's romances, my father's school and college prizes, dignified books in whole calf and in pigskin, adorned with the arms of Cowbridge School and Jesus College, Oxford, in rich gold. Here was the Judicious Hooker, whose judiciousness, I regret to say, I could never abide nor stomach; here that noble book, Parker's "Glossary of Gothic Architecture," in three volumes, one of text and two of beautifully executed plates; and here was an early volume of Tennyson.

Of these two last-named books I can scarcely say which is the more precious and eminent in my recollection. The one stands for my initiation into the spirit of Gothic, and I think that is one of the most magical of all initiations. More furious and frantic nonsense has been talked about "paganism" than about almost any other subject; it will only be necessary to think of Swinburne with his "world has grown grey" phrase to indicate what manner of nonsense I have in mind. But the fact is that the heart of paganism was not exactly contrite or broken, but certainly resigned, with an austere and stoical acceptance of fate, which is not without its beauty and its majesty. The nearest modern equivalent to the classic or pagan spirit is Calvinism — the Oedipus Tyrannus is nothing but the doctrine of predestination set to solemn music — and this aus-

tere spirit stamped itself on all the finest Greek art. It
is somewhat softened in Plato, for Plato drew from the
East by way of Pythagoras, but the beauty of Greek
tragedy, architecture, sculpture, is essentially austere
and severe. It is Calvinism in marble; and judgment
and inexorable vengeance on guilty sinners are sung
in choral odes.

Now winter has its splendors; but with what joy do
we welcome the yearly miracle of spring. We and the
whole earth exult together as though we had been
delivered from prison, the hedgerows and the fields are
glad, and the woods are filled with singing; and men's
hearts are filled with an ineffable rapture. Israel once
more has come out of Egypt, from the house of bondage. And all this is expressed in the Gothic, and much
more than this. It is the art of the supreme exaltation,
of the inebriation of the body and soul and spirit of
man. It is not resigned to dwell calmly, stoically, aus-
terely on the level plains of this earthly life, since its
joy is in this, that it has stormed the battlements of
heaven. And so its far-lifted vaults and its spires rush
upward, and its pinnacles are like a wood of springing
trees. And its hard stones, its strong-based pillars break
out as it were into song, they blossom as the rose; all
the secrets of the garden and the field and the wood
have been delivered unto them. And not only is all this
true of building. Take a common iron nail that is to
be driven into a door. The Gothic smith would so deal
with that nail that its head should become a little piece
of joy and fantasy, a little portion of paradise. Nay,
take the letter A, as the Romans gave it to us; a plain,
well-built, businesslike letter, admirably fulfilling its
purpose, with no nonsense about it. Now look at a
thirteenth-century illuminated manuscript and seek
out this A. It has every kind of "nonsense" about it; of
that nonsense that makes earth into heaven. It is not

only that it glows with rich raised gold, that it is most imperially vested in blue and in scarlet, but its frigid form has relaxed into beauty; it is no longer a mere letter, it is as a wild rose tree in a hedge. From it spring curves of infinite grace, which enclose the page of text, and hair-line branches break from the main stem and blossom out into flowers of paradise: so the wild roses, delicate, enchanting, sway and quiver over the green field in the month of June.

So much for the "Glossary"; now for the other volume, the little early Tennyson. My attention was directed to this in an odd manner. One of the masters at school had called me a "lotus-eater," and I was much pleased with the sound of the phrase, though the master did not mean to be complimentary, and I had no notion as to what a lotus-eater really was. But in the course of the next holidays, rummaging at random among the books at the rectory, as my custom was, I opened the Tennyson and found the poem of "The Lotos-Eaters" with the "Choric Song" annexed. I began to read that I might be instructed as to the exact nature of my crime. I read on, enchanted, and it was then, in my twelfth or thirteenth year, that I first delighted in poetry as poetry, for its own sake, apart from any story it might tell.

And here I find an extraordinary difficulty in "making a distinction," as the casuists say, between two very different kinds of literary pleasure. For some time I had enjoyed great literature in such books as "Don Quixote" and Sir Walter Scott's romances; but "The Lotos-Eaters" — which is also, I think, great literature — gave me a quite new and peculiar delight. Hitherto it had been the story which had charmed me; but now I found myself delighting in the music and melody of verse, in the "atmosphere" of the poem, in the "color" of the words — to use terms of which I disapprove, but for which I can find no efficient substitutes. I suspect, indeed, that I found in Tennyson's poem the transmuted and golden image of my own solitary and meditative habit of mind; and this may have counted for something in the sum of my delight. The master, a cheery, excellent young man as I remember him, may have made a correct diagnosis; I had been a lotus-eater for years without knowing it, and so recognized Ulysses' entranced companions as my true comrades in dreams. It may have been so; but in any case I have always dated my inoculation with the specific virus of literature from my reading of those verses in the little calf-bound volume.

Chapter III

Some years ago I was asked by the editor of a well-known paper to write a short series of articles about London. The subject seems ambitious enough, and indeed London considered either physically or intellectually is so vast and mighty a world, that the study of any one — of even the smallest and least considerable — of its aspects may well be the task of a lifetime. But, so far as I can remember, my instructions were of the

liberal and catholic kind. I mean, I was not required
to write of the great city as the goal of the timber
merchant or of the dealer in precious stones, or of the
makers of chasubles, or of the fashioner of wigs, but
rather to depict it as the end sought by all these, and
by myriads more. And so I set about the task in my
usual spirit, firmly convinced, that is, that better men
had said all that there was to say on the matter brought
before me, and yet resolved to do my best and to try
to make something of the job in one way or another.
So I set to work, and found, strangely enough, that
though I was writing about London, I was also writing
a mystical treatise, on a text which I will not divulge
in this place. But for the beginning of my series I
remember that I went back a good many years to the
time when London began to call to me. I often speculate now in these later days as to how it would have
been with me if this call had never come. For I have
certain friends — very few of them — still living in
Gwent and on its borders who have not heard the
summons. The special family that I have in mind has
lived in those regions for more centuries than I can
tell. It would be a bold and learned Welsh herald who
would trace them to their beginnings on the Celtic
side, but on the Norman they go back to Sir Payne
Turberville, the companion of Fitzhamon, and even
in Wales a story of nine hundred years is a long story.

Well, coming down a little through the ages, the
Rowlands that I knew — of course, their grandfather
knew my grandfather — are still on the soil. Certainly
a younger son has crossed the Severn, but the two
others have not moved their habitations more than ten
or twelve miles in the last fifty years. From halfway
between Newport and Cardiff to Newport, from Newport to a mile east of Newport, then to four miles east
of Newport, at last to three miles west of Cardiff: they

will surely be laid in the land of their fathers at the end. So it might have been with me, perhaps, if it had not been for the blood of certain Scottish sailors intermingled with the stay-at-home stock of Gwent. But I often wonder, as I say, how it would have happened to me if I had found a home under the shadow of Twyn Barlwm instead of becoming a dweller in the tents of London. Tents, I say advisedly, for, with the rarest exceptions, Londoners have no homes. This was true in a great measure nearly two hundred years ago, when Dr. Johnson first came to London from Lichfield; it is now all but universally true.

But, anyhow, the call of London, partly external and partly internal, came to me, and for some months before I left the old land for the first time I was imagining London and making a picture of it in my mind, and longing for it. I turned up the old magazines and re-read Sala's "Twice Round the Clock." I came upon the strange phrase, "the City," in stories, and wondered what the City signified. And I began to have an appetite for London papers. For it should be understood that at Llanddewi Rectory a London paper was a thing of the rarest appearance. I think I can remember that when the Prince of Wales — afterwards King Edward VII, of happy memory — was dangerously ill, my father made some kind of arrangement — I cannot think what it could have been — by which he got the "Echo" of those days, not only on week days, but on Sunday afternoons. And in ordinary times, when we went into Newport on market days, we might possibly bring back a "Standard" or a "Telegraph," but likely enough not. We saw the "Western Mail" occasionally, the "Hereford Times" once a week; weekly also came the "Guardian," an excellent paper, but with more of Oxford, Pater, and Freeman, and Deans, and Dignitaries in it than of London or Londoners. Indeed, I remember how the news of the fall of Khartoum came to the rectory. I had been spending the evening with some friends across a few miles of midnight and black copse, and ragged field and wild, broken, and wandering brook land, and I remember that not a star was to be seen as I came home, wondering all the while if I ever should find my way. One of my friends had been in Newport that day, and had seen a paper, and so when I got back at last and found my father smoking his pipe by the fire, I announced the news in a tag of Apocalyptic Greek: Khartoum he polis he megale pep-toke, peptoke; Khartoum the mighty city, has fallen, has fallen. And sometimes I wonder now in these days, when I am nearer to the heart of newspapers, whether our work in Fleet Street, with its anxious, flurried yell over the telephone, its tic-tac of tapes, its slither and rattle and clatter of linotypes, its frantic haste of men, its final roar and thunder of machinery ever gets itself delivered at last on a midnight hillside so queerly as the tragic news of Khartoum was delivered in the "parlor" of Llanddewi Rectory.

But the days came when above the clear voice of the brook in the hidden valley, above the murmur of the trees in the heart of the greenwood there sounded from beyond the hills to my heart a clearer voice, a mightier murmur. London called me, and all documents relating to this new unknown world became matters of the highest consequence and significance, and so London papers must by all means be obtained.

Far and long ago that spring and summer of 1880 now seem to me. It was then that London began to summon, and I was filled with an eager curiosity to know all about the new world which I was to visit.

As I have explained, the London paper made a very rare and occasional appearance at Llanddewi-among-the-Hills, and I don't think that any of us felt any aching need of it. But now for me "Standard" and "Telegraph" became mystic documents of the highest interest and most vital consequence; these were the charts to the Nova Terra Incognita; every line in them came from the heart of the mystery and was written by men who were learned in all the wisdom of London. London papers I must have; that was certain; so I set out to get them.

The nearest point at which these precious rarities were obtainable was Pontypool Road Station, about four miles distant from Llanddewi Rectory. It was the place where I had bought my copy of "De Quincey" some years earlier, and is now sacred to me on that account. But in this month of April thirty-five years ago I thought little of De Quincey or of his visions. Columbus, I suspect, while he watched the fitting of his caravel forgot any mere literary enthusiasms that he might have once possessed; for him there was but one object and that was the tremendous, marvelous, terrible venture into the unknown that he was soon to make. So it was with me; London loomed up before me, wonderful, mystical as Assyrian Babylon, as full of unheard-of things and great unveilings as any magic city in an Eastern tale. It loomed up with incredible pinnacles — to quote Tennyson on another city — and in its mighty shadow all lesser objects disappeared. De Quincey? After all he was not without value, since he spoke of Oxford Street; still, I wanted later news of the City of the Enchanters. So three or four times a week I walked the four miles to Pontypool Road, taking the short cut across the fields which leaves the byway at Croeswen and brings one out on the high road from Newport to Abergavenny, somewhere about a mile from the station, near the lane which wanders through a very solitary country into Usk.

Pontypool Road Station lies, as I have said, under mountains, or rather under the huge domed hills which we in Gwent call mountains. It is one of the many meeting-points between the fields and the "works," and is always associated in my mind with a noise of clanking machinery and a reek of black oily smoke of rich flavor, which this generation would not recognize, since it is only to be imitated by blowing out a tallow candle that has long wanted snuffing; and now there are neither tallow candles nor snuffers. Here, then, of a "celestial" agent of W. H. Smith I bought my papers; usually the "Standard" and the "Daily Telegraph." The "Morning Post" was, I think, twopence in those days, and twopence was too much to give for a daily paper, and, moreover, we had a vague belief that the "Morning Post" was almost exclusively concerned with the social doings of the aristocracy, splendid matters, doubtless, but no affairs of mine. With these two papers, then, and once a week with a copy of "Truth," I would make my way out of the station, and along the high road till I came to the stile and the lonely path across the fields, and alone under a tree or in the shelter of a friendly hedge I would open my papers, cut their pages, and plunge into their garden of delights. One of my chief interests in these journals — perhaps my chiefest interest — was the theater; and I am sure I cannot say why this was so. As far as I can remember I had up to this time witnessed three performances of stage plays, and of these three one was certainly not "legitimate," being a drama of the circus called "Dick Turpin's Ride to York." Its chief incidents were firing pistols and leaping over five-barred gates, and I must have been about seven when I saw it at Cardiff. Then in '76 I was at Dublin, and saw "Our Boys," and was very heartily bored, and finally in '78 or '79 I went with a school-fellow to the skating-rink at Hereford — I remember the former as well as the latter rinking mania — and enjoyed a touring company's rendering of "Pinafore." And, looking back, I believe that it was then that the delightful poison began to work; then when in that ramshackle barn of a place in the Hereford backstreet the curtain went up on the Saturday afternoon, and eight men dressed as sailors began to sing: —

We sail the ocean blue,
    And our saucy ship's a beauty;
We're gallant men and true,
    And attentive to our duty.

I remember that, young as I was, I could not help feeling that eight was a very small number for the male chorus. This circumstance confirms me in a belief which I have long entertained that Heaven meant me to be a stage-manager. True, I could never master simple addition, and a stage-manager has to keep accounts. Still, I should not have been the first stage-manager whose ledgers were filled with "comptes fantastiques."

But here I am under my tree or my hedge on a sunny morning of that Gwentian spring of so many years ago, eagerly opening the paper and turning to the theatrical advertisements in that part of the journal which I have in later years learned to call the "leader page." I read about Mr. Henry Irving at the Lyceum and Mr. Toole at the Folly — I do not think the vanished theater was known as Toole's in those days. Mme. Modjeska and Mr. Forbes-Robertson were, I believe, at the Court, Dion Boucicault's play, "The Shaughraun," was running at the Adelphi — or, stay, was this old house of melodrama then the home of "The Danites?" In Wych Street, at the Opera Comique, was "The Pirates of Penzance"; "Madame Favart" enchanted at the Strand;

"Les Cloches de Corneville" was at the Globe or the
Olympic, I forget which. And, said each advertisement,
"for cast see under the clock."

I was vividly interested in that phrase, "For cast see
under the clock," which I read in the sibylline leaves
of my London papers. The real meaning of the words
never occurred to me; I conceived that somewhere, in
some dimly-imagined central place of London, there
was a great clock on a high square tower, and that this
tower was so prominent an architectural feature as to
be known all over London as "the clock." And at the
base of this tower, so I proceeded in my fancy, there
were displayed bills or posters, containing the casts of
all the plays of all the theaters. I never found that
mighty tower in London, but it was many years before
it dawned on me that "the clock" was merely the
pictured clock-face in the newspaper itself, under
which the full casts were then printed.

As I have said, I cannot quite make out the sources
of this intense interest of mine in the theater. But I
suspect that for the time I had got into that strange
frame of mind to which Thackeray alluded when he
asked a man if he were "fond of the play." Thackeray's
friend replied, I think, to the effect that it depended
on the play, whereupon Thackeray told him that he
didn't understand in the least what the phrase "fond
of the play" implied. Thackeray was right; for this
attitude of mind is universal, not particular; and oddly
enough, I believe it is very little related to any serious
interest in the drama as a form of art. There is so vast
a gulf between the theater of today and that of thirty-
five years ago that I do not know whether it is now
possible for anybody to be "fond of the play" in the

old sense; but if there be such people left, I am sure that they have not the faintest interest in the proposals to build and endow a national theater. For to those in the happy state to which Thackeray alluded, the theater was loved not for itself, but as a symbol of gaiety; I would almost say of metropolitanism as opposed to provincialism. I have known countrymen relating their adventures in London almost to wink as they included a visit to the Globe or the Strand in the list of their pleasures; the theater represented to them the "chimes at midnight" mood.

Thackeray meant — do you like the mingled gas and orange odors of the theater, do you like the sound of the orchestra tuning, the sight of the footlights suddenly lightening, can you project your self readily into the fantastic world disclosed by the rising curtain, and afterwards, do you like a midnight chop at Evans's, with Welsh rarebit to follow, and foaming tankards of brown stout, and then "something hot"; in fine, do you like to be out and about and in the midst of gaiety at hours of the night when your uncles and aunts and all quiet country people are abed and fast asleep? That is what Thackeray meant by his question, and I suppose that our modern, serious lovers of the drama would regard the man who was fond of the play in this sense as an utter reprobate, a stumbling-block and a stone of offence. But it was in that sense that I pored devoutly over everything relating to the theater that I found in my newspapers, as I delayed in my walks home from Pontypool Road, not being able to refrain any longer.

Well, the day dawned at last for dreams to come true — or as true as they ever come. My father and I set out one fine Monday morning for Paddington, starting, I think, at about eleven o'clock from Newport, and getting to London by five in the afternoon. This was then the best train in the day; for the Severn Tunnel

was not yet made, and we went all the way round by
Gloucester. It was a six hours' journey, and now one
can get from London to Newport in two hours and a
half. At Westbourne Park we changed and got into the
Underground system, and so came to the Temple Station on the Embankment. Thence it was a short walk
to the private hotel in Surrey Street where my father
had always stayed on his infrequent visits to town. I
have forgotten the name of the hotel; — Bradshaw's
office is built on the site of it — it was Williams's, or
Smith's, or Evans's, or some such title, and as I believe
was then the way, it was understood to be more or less
the preserve of people from the west. I suppose there
were other little hotels for parsons and small squires
of the east and north and south; for all the streets that
go down from the Strand to the river were then occupied by these private hotels and by lodging-houses.
Craven Street, by Charing Cross, is the only one of
these streets that has at all preserved the old manner,
which, let me say, was a dingy and dim but on the
whole a comfortable manner. Our hotel was just opposite the pit door of the old Strand Theatre, and in a
former visit my father and mother, sitting at their
window, had had the gratification of seeing Mrs. Swan-
borough sitting at her window over the way knitting
busily. Now all our ladies, however smart, have become
knitters, but if I had been writing these reminiscences
a few years ago I should have asked: "Can you imagine
a London manageress of these days sitting and knitting
in her room at the theater?"

We went out for a short stroll before eating, and for
the first time I saw the Strand, and it instantly went to
my head and to my heart, and I have never loved
another street in quite the same way. My Strand is gone
forever; some of it is a wild rock-garden of purple
flowers, some of it is imposing new buildings; but one

way or another, the spirit is wholly departed. But on that June night in 1880 I walked up Surrey Street and stood on the Strand pavement and looked before me and to right and to left and gasped. No man has ever seen London; but at that moment I was very near to the vision — the *theoria* — of London.

After the astounding glimpse at the Strand we went back to the private hotel in Surrey Street and had something to eat. I am not sure, but I think the meal consisted of tea and ham and eggs, the latter beautifully poached. I know that my mind holds a recollection of this simple dish very admirably done in connection with Smith's, or whatever the place was called; and I believe it was eaten in the evening of our arrival. And I may say in passing that the hotel had a pleasant, well-worn, homely look about it; very plain, but extremely comfortable. I think that my bedroom carpet was threadbare and that the bed was a feather bed; at all events one slept sublimely there under the roof, under the London stars.

Then for the Strand again, now sunset flushed, beginning to twinkle with multitudinous lamps — I had hardly seen a lamp-lit street before — and so to the Opéra Comique, where they were playing "The Pirates of Penzance." The Opéra Comique was somewhere in Wych Street, which has gone the way of the streets of Babylon and Troy; purple blossoms and big hotels and other theaters that I know not grow now in the place where it once stood. We went to the upper boxes of the Opéra Comique and enjoyed ourselves very well. I remember my father being especially pleased with the Pirate King's defense of his profession: "Compared with respectability it's almost honest," or words to that effect. But, oddly enough, I was a little disappointed. There was not the sense of gaiety that I had expected. For one thing the music reminded me of the classic glees and madrigals which I had heard discoursed by the Philharmonic Society at Hereford, where I was at school, and I did not want to be reminded of Hereford. And the female chorus hardly looked as thoughtless as I could have wished; it seemed to me that they might very well have come fresh from the rectory like myself. Of course, it was all very well to be ladylike, and so forth; but what I asked of the stage was careless devilry, the suggestion, at all events, of naughtiness. In fact, my attitude was perilously near to that of the Arkansas audiences as analyzed by the Duke in "Huckleberry Finn": "What they wanted was low comedy — and maybe something ruther worse than low comedy." But I was not really quite so bad as the "Arkansaw lunk-heads." We went on another night to "Les Cloches de Corneville," a most harmless production, I am sure; and *that* was what I wanted. I was enchanted from the rising of the curtain; there was the sunlit scene in Normandy, charming, smiling, and a whole row of pretty girls, evidently as thoughtless as the lightest heart could wish, dancing down to the footlights and singing: —

        Just look at that,
        Just look at this,
Don't you think we're not amiss?
        A glance give here,
        A glance give there,
Tell us if you think we're dear.

And — not one of these girls looked as if she could have come from any conceivable rectory. Decidedly, "Les Cloches de Corneville" was the comic opera for my money. What a pleasing thrill the scene afforded when the entire village, for some reason that I cannot well remember, dressed up as Crusaders and Crusaderesses, and came suddenly into the room of Gaspard, the miser, and the big bell began to toll and the gold was poured out in a torrent on the ground. "When the heir returneth, then shall ring the bell, so the legend runneth, so the old men tell"; in some such words was this grand peripeteia announced in the text. So the heir no doubt returned and married the extra pretty girl whose name I have forgotten — she was not Serpolette, I know, for Serpolette was comic, delightfully, impudently comic, but still comic, and so no mate for the hero. Serpolette, I think, having regard to the Unities, ought to have married the thin but amusing assistant of the Bailie; but I do not know whether this were so. But I am sure everybody was happy ever after, and of "Les Cloches" and other comic operas like it I say, in the words of Coleridge's friend: "Them's the jockeys for me!"

I have never been able to make up my mind as to the respective merits of "Les Cloches de Corneville" and "Madame Favart," which was running at the Strand. "Les Cloches" had the more coherent plot of the two, and the great scene of the miser and the crusaders was more effective in its stagey way than anything in "Madame Favart," but, then, Florence St. John was Madame Favart, and to old playgoers I need say no more. And Marius, a delightful French comedian, was in the cast; and there were those songs dear to memory: "Ave, my mother," "The Artless Thing," "To Age's Dull December," and

Pair of lovers meet,
Stolen vows are sweet,
Sighs, etcetera.
Love is all in all,
On a garden wall,
Never heed papa.

This was sung by Marius, who had no voice in particular, but an infinite Gallic relish and unction and finish in everything that he did. The fourth piece that we went to in this wonderful week was "The Daughter of the Drum Major," at the Alhambra, then a theater, with an extremely roomy, comfortable pit. This last piece made but little impression on me. From my recollection, it seems to have been more in the modern mode, that is, a mere excuse for showing off a "beauty chorus" without the little touch of thin, theatrical but pleasant romance that delighted me in the two other plays. But the poverty of the play was atoned for by the happy circumstance that before going to it we dined at the Cavour. And the Cavour in 1880 was exactly like the Cavour in 1915, save in this one matter, that on the earlier date there was included in the price of the dinner a bottle of violet wine.

*L*ooking back through the years and comparing the London of the early 'eighties with the London of today, one circumstance emerges very clearly in my mind: that is, that the early London had an infinitely "smarter," wealthier air than the later. I say "air" advisedly, to make it clear that I knew nothing of the real interior life of the place, or of the resources of its rich inhabitants. I judged of London purely by its exterior aspects, as one may judge of a passing stranger in the street, and decide that he goes to an expensive tailor, without knowing anything of the condition of his banking account. So, I say that the outward show and lineaments of the London of 1880 were much more refulgent and splendid than those of the last few years.

I was a good deal surprised when the truth of this first dawned on me some three or four years ago. For I believe that as a matter of fact the new London is a much wealthier, more luxurious, more extravagant place than the old. The rich people of today spend hundreds instead of tens, thousands for the hundreds of their fathers; the "pace" of the splendid has increased enormously in the last thirty-five years; and all the facilities for expending very large sums of money have also increased to a huge extent. So well was I convinced of all this when I fell to comparing the London of my boyhood with the London of my middle age that at first I thought that there must be a fallacy somewhere, and I was very willing to believe that those early impressions of mine were illusions, natural enough in a lad who had never seen anymore splendid streets than those which the Newport and Cardiff of those days had to show, than the venerable, peaceful, ancient ways of Hereford, whose stillness was only broken by the deep, sweet chiming of the cathedral bells. But when, interested, I went into the facts of the question, I found that I had not been mistaken in my first view — i.e., that London was a smarter-looking place thirty years ago than at the present day, and this for several reasons.

To begin with, there is the trifling matter of men's dress. I do not know whether we have yet realized the fact that the frock coat is rapidly becoming "costume," verging, that is, towards the status of levee dress. Already, I believe, it is only worn on occasions of semi-state, at functions where the King is expected, at smart weddings, and so forth. Before long it will probably attain the singular twofold state of "evening dress," which is worn all day long by waiters and by what are conveniently called gentlemen after seven o'clock in the evening. So very likely the frock coat will soon be seen on the backs of the maître d'hôtel, the hotel manager, the shopwalker, the major-domo — if there be any majores-domo left — as a kind of uniform or livery, while it will also be the afternoon wear of dukes at great social functions. And so with the silk hat; it has not gone so far on the road of obsolescence as the frock coat, but, unless I mistake, it has entered on that sad way.

Here, then, is the point of contrast. Between 'eighty and 'ninety — and later still — practically every man in London went about his business and his pleasure with a high hat on his head. Every man, I say, above the rank of the mechanic; certainly all the clerkly class; Mr. Guppy and his friends were still faithful to this head-dress; which, be it remembered, was once universal all over England, so that even smock-frocked farm labor-ers wore it. As for the London of pleasure, the West End, it would have been quite impossible to conceive a man of the faintest social pretensions being seen abroad in anything else. And now, I go up and down Piccadilly, Bond Street, the Row at the height of the London season, and see — a few silk hats and morning coats, it is true — but the majority of well-dressed men in "lounge" suits and grey soft hats and black and grey bowlers.

Now let it be clearly understood that I have no passion for black coats and shiny hats myself, nor for the dazzling white linen which has largely given way to soft, unstarched stuffs. But it is not to be denied that all those habits had a "smart" appearance, and that a pavement crowded with shiny black hats, shiny white cuffs and collars, and long black frock coats made a much more imposing show than the pavement of today, on which the men's dress is very much as they please. The modern men look extremely comfortable and well at their ease; but they do not scintillate in the old style. A soft grey hat does not flash back the rays of the sun.

Then, another point and a most important one: the coming of the motor. I suppose the kind of motor-impelled vehicle which one is likely to see in Hyde Park may very well have cost seven or eight or nine or ten times as much as the horse-drawn carriages which I remember going round and round so gay and so glorious. Well, I have watched the modern procession of motorcars, and they are about as impressive as a career of light locomotive engines. It may indeed in course of time become fashionable to go up and down the Row in express locomotives capable of drawing their hundred coaches at a hundred miles an hour, but the effect would not be smart. Now, the old equipages were undeniably the last word of smartness; in themselves they were enough to tell the stranger that he had come to the very center of the earth, of its riches and its splendors. There were the highbred, high-spirited, high-stepping horses, in the first place, groomed to the last extreme of shiny, satiny perfection, tossing their heads proudly and champing their bits and doing the most wonderful things with their legs. The bright sunlight of those past London summers shone on their glossy coats, shone in the patent leather of the harness, shone and glittered on the plated bolts and buckles and ornaments. And the carriages were of graceful form, and the servants of those days sometimes wore gorgeous liveries; and scores of those brilliant equipages followed on one another in an unending dazzling procession. That was the old way; now there are some "Snorting Billies" that choke and snarl and splutter as they dodge furtively and meanly in and out of the Park, like mechanical rabbits bolting for their burrows.

While I contrast the London of my young days and the London of my old — or present — days, I would like it to be remembered that I am, so far, only contrasting the two cities from one point of view, the point of view of smartness. I have not been saying that 1880 London was more sensible than 1915 London; but merely that the former struck an outsider as a more brilliant place than the modern city. The fact is that I have the most cordial approval for all social pomps and splendors, so long as I am not required to take part therein. I hate wearing frock coats and silk hats and shiny shirts; but I am very well pleased to sit in the pit, as it were, and watch those exalted persons who are cast for the decorative parts going through their brilliant performances. And, after all, if a man finds that plate armor is uncomfortable, that is no reason why he should not delight in seeing other people wearing it, and wearing it with dignity. And in speaking of the Hyde Park and Rotten Row of the old days I mentioned that there were some gorgeous servants' liveries still left in 1880. And while we are on that matter, I may say that I have never sympathized at all with those persons who have found something mean and ridiculous in a manservant in purple and gold or in blue and crimson, unless, that is, the point be taken that only a splendid duty should be dignified with a splendid vestment, and in that objection I admit there is some force. Not that I agree for one moment that there is anything contemptible in "menial" service; but I am willing to allow that it may not be altogether seemly for a faithful fellow, whose business is to hold on behind a carriage and wait at dinner, to outshine a bishop in pontificals. But I suspect that the people who sneered at poor Jeames and his plush were not actuated by this reasonable motive, but rather by that vile "Liberal" objection to splendor as splendor. The man who found "Blazes" ridiculous would probably find the King in his Coronation robes equally ridiculous. And so you may go on, up the scale and down the scale; but the only logical alternative to splendor is Dr. Johnson's proposed suit of bull's hide — all beyond that is super-fluity and vain show, according to the doctrine of the wretches who in times not long past sold antique civic ornaments, such as chains and maces, on the ground that the Mayor of Little Pedlington did not need such gauds to help him in his customary task of sentencing "drunks."

There is one more point in connection with the Row. Twenty-five years ago the appointed hour was five o'clock in the afternoon. Then people sat in the chairs and walked up and down and looked at the carriages, and I remember a friend observing to me this singu-larity, that though the place was public and open to anybody, still only those persons who were dressed in the regulation costume — frock coat and silk hat for men — ever came near the sacred ground. The people in lounge suits and bowler hats stood apart, and watched the show from some distance. Well, the hour of the Row is now in the morning; but there is a greater change. There are still "smart" people there; but there are also people who cannot by any possibility be de-scribed as smart, not even if they be judged by the very lax standards of these days.

In another matter the London of today is much less impressive in its outward show than the London of 1880; that is in the aspect of its principal streets. There are still excellent shops in Bond Street, Regent Street, and Piccadilly; but there is no longer in any of them that air of exclusiveness and expensiveness that I can remember, and this is particularly true of Regent Street. In 1880 you felt as soon as you turned up the Quadrant that anything you might buy therein would certainly

be dear; the very stones and stucco exuded costliness
and the essential attars of luxury. I feel convinced that
the cigars of Regent Street were of a more curious
aroma than cigars bought in any other street, that it
was the very place wherein to purchase a great green
flagon of rare scent as a present for a lady, that if you
happened to want a Monte Cristo emerald this was the
quarter wherein to search for it. That was my impression, but lest it should be mere fancy, a year or so ago
I asked one of the older shopkeepers whether the street
was quite what he and I remembered it. He said very
emphatically it was not at all what it had been; and I
feel sure that he was right, and that in a less degree the
other principal shopping centers have declined from
their former splendor.

And this for two reasons; first, the curious modern
tendency of the best and most luxurious shops to
scatter and disperse themselves abroad about the side
streets of the West End, leaving gaps which are filled
in most cases by dealers in cheaper wares. And secondly, the coming of the popular tea-shop has, in my
opinion, done a very great deal to "unsmarten" the
streets of which I am speaking. Let it not be understood
for one moment that I would speak despitefully of
cheap tea-shops; that would indeed be vilely thankless
in one who has often made the principal meal of the
day at an A.B.C. — large coffee, threepence; milk cake,
twopence; butter, a penny — and has been grateful that
for once in a way he has dined. But, it cannot be
pretended that a milk cake is a costly or a curious dish,
or that a plate of cold meat for sixpence or eightpence
is an opimian banquet; and so, when I pass a popular
tea-shop or eating-house, I feel that my dream of luxury
and expense is broken; and that something of glitter
and splendor has passed away from the West End of
London.

I spent the years from the summer of 1880 to the winter of 1886 in a singular sort of apprenticeship to life and London and letters and to most other things. Sometimes I was in London; then for months at a time I was out of it, back again in my old haunts of Gwent. I had hot fits of desire for the town when I was forced to stay in the country; and then, settled, or apparently settled, in the heart of London, its immensities and its solitudes overwhelmed me, the faint, hot breath of its streets sickened me, so that my heart ached for the thought of the green wood by the valley of the Soar, and for the thought of friendly faces.

They say that in old Japan they had a wonderful and secret art of tempering their sword blades. Now the steel was placed in the white heat of the fire, now it was withdrawn and plunged into the water of an icy torrent; and then again the trial of the furnace. So heat and cold were alternated, according to an ancient and hidden tradition, till at last the craftsman obtained an exquisite and true and perfect blade, fit for the adorned scabbard of a great lord of Japan. When I think of those early years of mine I should be reminded of the process of the Japanese sword-craftsman — if only the heart were as tractable as steel. The Kabbalists, I believe, take the view — a gloomy one — that the innermost essence of man's spirit goes out from the world in much the same state as that in which it came into the world; and it is certainly true that some men seem incorrigible; neither fire nor ice will temper them aright.

During these early years of my London experience I lived under very varying conditions. I lived with families, and I lived alone; I lived in the suburbs and in the center; I had enough to eat, and then narrowly escaped starvation. My first habitat was in the High Street of a southern suburb. My memory holds a picture of an ancient street of dignified red-brick houses, a Georgian church, and a stream of quite inky blackness. The old houses had old gardens behind them, green enough, but with a certain grime upon them that made them strange to eyes unused to this combination of soot and leafage. But it was quite easy in those days to get from the suburb to the open country.

Not that I desired any such excursions, for my notion of an ideal residence was then a lodging in one of the streets or courts or passages going down from the Strand to the Thames. This was a dream that I realized years afterwards, when many waters (not of the Thames) had passed over my head. It was well enough, and I used to go out and get my breakfast at the "chocolate as in Spain" shop at the west end of the Strand, on the north side. It was well enough, I say, but it was not absolute paradise. And, furthermore, and in an interior parenthesis, let me say that the chocolate at the old Strand shop was not as in Spain, though very decent chocolate. The Spanish service of chocolate — I encountered it when I was in Gasçony — consists in this, first that the chocolate is made extremely strong and thick, and secondly that with it comes a goblet of ice-cold well-water, to be drunk after the chocolate, on the principle, I suppose, of the Scots who drink water, not with whisky, but after it.

Well, to return to the more or less — chiefly less — direct current of my tale, after my sojourn in the southern suburb came a return to the country, where I remained eight or nine months. It was during this exodus or hegira, I think, that I was excommunicated by old Mr. James, of Lansoar, because I was loafing at home instead of living on five shillings a week in London. But my long sojourn in Gwent was in fact due to a very dismal discovery having been made of me by certain persons called examiners. They found me utterly incapable of the simple rules of arithmetic; and hence I was debarred from the career which I had been contemplating. And here I would say that I am almost proud of myself for my quite extraordinary arithmetical incapacity. I am not merely dull and slow, but desperate. I am so wanting in the mere faculty of counting as to be curious, like those tribes of savages that can say "One, two, three, four, five . . . many." There are people who make a living by exhibiting their arithmetical skill in the music halls; someone writes on the blackboard a multiplication sum of fifteen figures multiplied by fifteen figures, and a second or two after the last figure is drawn the arithmetical artist utters the result. Well, I am at the opposite end of the scale, and I have sometimes wondered whether "Incompetent Machen" would not be quite a good turn. It would make anybody laugh to hear me doing a sum in simple addition. It is like "Forty-seven and nine, forty-seven and nine, forty-seven and nine." I ponder. Then a brilliant idea strikes me. I pretend the problem is "forty-seven and ten." I get the result, fifty-seven, deduct one and proceed.

Well, I came to London again in the summer of '81, thinking of another and quite a different career, which did not involve, on the face of it, that little difficulty of arithmetic. Again I was in a suburb, and again in an old one, but this time the quarter was in the far west. I stayed in Turnham Green, then a place of many amenities standing amongst fields and gardens and riparian lawns, which, long ago, have been buried beneath piles of cheap bricks and mortar, for a year and a half, and then again I altered my plans, or fate rather altered them for me. I started on a new tack and kept it for a month, and then somehow slid into a backwater, in which I was afloat and nothing more than afloat. Summoning this period into recollection,

I find my position very much like to that of certain ancient and outworn barges, grass-grown, flower-grown, that I have come upon suddenly in improbable back alleys of water, in the midst of a maze of by-streets at Brentford; but, locally and literally, I was then living in a small room, a very small room, in Clarendon Road, Notting Hill Gate.

I have already stated that when I first came up to London I had no thought of literature as a career. Indeed, I never have thought of it as a career, but only as a destiny. Still, my meaning is that it in no wise dawned upon me as I traveled up from Newport to London in the early summer of 1880 that writing of any kind or sort was to be a great part of my life's business. And yet, before I had lived a month in the old red house by the inky stream, I was trying to write, in the intervals of a very different task, in an atmosphere which was utterly remote from literature of any kind. How was this? Partly, I suppose, because of the very large proportion of Celtic blood in my veins. It is quite true that the Celt — the Welsh Celt, at all events — has directly contributed very little to great literature. This I have always maintained, and always shall maintain; and I think all impartial judges will allow that if Welsh literature were annihilated at this moment the loss to the world's grand roll of masterpieces would be insignificant. I, speaking from the point of view of my own peculiar interests, I should be very sorry to miss my copy of the "Mabinogion," and there are certain stanzas of the poem called "Y Beddau" — "Vain is it to seek for the grave of Arthur" — which have a singular and enchanting and wizard music; but in neither case is there any question of a literary masterpiece.

Yet there is in Celtdom a certain literary feeling which does not exist in Anglo-Saxondom. It is diffused, no doubt, and appreciative rather than creative, and lacking in the sterner, critical spirit which is so necessary to all creative work; still it is there, and it is delighted with the rolling sound of the noble phrase. It perceives the music of words and the relation of that music to the world. I was taking a lesson in Welsh pronunciation some time ago, and uttered the phrase "yn oes oesodd" — from ages to ages. "That is right," said my Welsh friend, "speak it so that it makes a sound like the wind about the mountains." And, with or without the leave of the literary rationalists, I would say that the spirit of that sentence is very near to the heart of true literature.

So far then, as a man three-parts Celt, I was by nature inclined to the work of words, and there was, moreover, a feeble literary strain in my own family. There was a second cousin, or Welsh uncle, I am not certain which, who had composed a five-act heroic blank verse drama, called "Inez de Castro," which was almost, but not quite, represented by the famous Mrs. Somebody at the Lane in the early 'fifties. And then, more potent still, was the heredity of bookishness, the growing up among books that had accrued from grandfathers and uncles and cousins, all men who had lived all their days amongst books, and had sat over country hearths on mountain sides, reading this leathern Colloquies of Erasmus, this little Horace in mellow parchment, with the Sphere of Elzevir.

And then there was the old-fashioned grammar school education, of which it must be said, by friends and foes, that it is an education in words. One spent one's time, unconsciously, in weighing the values of words in English and Greek and Latin, in rendering one tongue into another, in estimating the exact sense of an English sentence before translating it into one or another of the old tongues. So that a boy who could do decent Latin prose must first have mastered the exact sense and significance of his English original, and then he must also have made himself understand to a certain extent, not only the logic but the polite habit of each language. I remember when I was a very small boy rendering "Put to the sword" literally into "Gladio positi." "Well," said my master, "there is no reason on earth why the Romans shouldn't have said 'gladio positi,' but as a matter of fact they *did* say 'ferro occisi' — killed with iron." And if one thinks of it, he who has mastered that little lesson has also mastered the larger lesson that literature is above logic, that there are matters in it which transcend plain common sense. And so, the long and the short of it was, that in 1880 I began to try to write.

Now I believe that one of the most tortuous and difficult questions that engages philosophy is the theory of cause and effect. I think, though I am not quite sure, that in one of Mr. Balfour's philosophical books this matter is treated, and the familiar case of a sportsman's pulling a trigger, firing a gun, and thereby bringing down a bird, is made an instance. What is the "cause" of the bird's death? Roughly speaking, of course, the pulling of the trigger; but roughly speaking is not the same thing as philosophically speaking; and if anyone be so simple as to conclude that roughly speaking means truly speaking and that philosophy is all nonsense, let me remind him that when he enjoys his after-dinner cigar in his armchair he is not conscious of the fact that he is being whirled through space, like a top, at the most terrific speed.

So, if I remember rightly, Mr. Balfour left the philosophical "cause" of the bird's death an open question, if not a question altogether beyond determination of human wit; and thus it is with the impulse that sends off a harmless young fellow on the career of letters. One can talk of the causes that impel a grain of corn to grow from the ground; sound seed, good soil, good farming; dry weather, wet weather, each in its season; but at the last the engendering of the green shoot remains a mystery. And so it is a mystery that near midsummer in 1880 I suddenly began to write horrible rubbish in a little manuscript book with a scarlet cover; rubbish that had rhymes to it.

But if ultimate causes lie beyond those flaming walls of the world that put bounds to all our inquisition, it is not so hard to trace those causes which are proximate. The bird dies because the shot hit it in a vital part, the corn sprouts because it is put into the ground — and I began to write because I bought a copy of Swinburne's "Songs Before Sunrise."

I forget how I heard of this name, which once loomed so fiery and strange a portent, which still, in the estimation of many excellent judges, stands for a great literary achievement. I know it was while I was down in the country, because I can remember one of our clergy, an Eton and Christchurch man, telling me gossip about the poet, who had in those early days retired from the world to Putney. It is to be supposed that I had read something concerning Swinburne in one of those wonderful London papers that came over our hills from another world, that might almost have fallen from the stars they were so wholly marvelous. But, somehow or other, I was possessed by an eager curiosity concerning this Swinburne, convinced in advance — I cannot remember how — that here I should surely find an unexpected, unsurmized treasure. And so, one hot, shiny afternoon, I came up from the old Georgian suburb by the black stream, crossed Hungerford Bridge, and made my way into the Strand; into that Strand which is as lost as Atlantis. And going eastward past many vanished things, past the rich odors of Messrs. Rimell's soap-boiling, I came to St.

Mary-le-Strand, and the entrance of Holywell Street. At the southern corner of this street, facing the east end of the church, there stood Denny's bookshop, and, gold in my pocket, I went in with a bold appearance, and said, "Have you got Swinburne's 'Songs Before Sunrise'?" The shopman did not seem in the least astonished at my question. He said he had got the book, and produced it, and showed it me, and the very cover was such as I had never seen before, provocative, therefore, in a high degree. And so I bought the book and carried it out of Denny's into the sunlight in a great amazement.

For, be it remembered, one did not go into a provincial bookshop in that easy way and say, "Have you got this or that?" For the chances were about a thousand to one that they hadn't got it, and never would have it. It is odd, but I cannot remember exactly the nature of the stock of the average country bookseller; my impression is of Bibles, Prayer Books, Church Services, and Pitman's Shorthand Manuals. So, if you wanted a book in the county town, you did not say, "Have you got so-and-so?" but "Will you get me so-and-so?" and in four or five days you called and the book was ready. But I had a notion that in this wonderful London the bookshop would actually have the book that you wanted, there actually in presence, and waiting for you on its shelves. I had a notion, I say, but again, it seemed almost incredible that there should be such shops in the world, and so when the bookseller under St. Mary-le-Strand said "Yes," quite simply, and handed me the "Songs Before Sunrise" in two or three seconds, I was amazed and exultant too; the legend of London, though marvelous, was evidently a true one.

Now I have a friend who is very fond of preaching the doctrine of what he calls the cataclysm. He holds that we are all much bettered by an occasional earth-

quake, moral, mental or spiritual. He says that volcanoes which suddenly burst out from under our feet are
the finest tonics in the world, that violent thunder-
storms, cloudbursts, and tornadoes clear our mental
skies. The treatment is heroic, but my friend may be
right; certainly that volume of "Songs Before Sunrise"
was to me quite cataclysmic. First there was the literary
manner of the book, which to me was wholly strange
and new and wonderful, and then there was the tremendous boldness of it all, the denial of everything
that I had been brought up to believe most sure and
sacred; the book was positively strewn with the fragments of shattered altars and the torn limbs of kings
and priests.

How do the lines go? I quote from memory, but they
run something like this: —

Thou hast taken all, Galilæan, but these thou shalt
      not take;
The laurel, the doves and the pæan, the breasts of
      the nymph in the brake.

Clearly this was a terrible, a tremendous fellow, an
earth-shaking, heaven-storming poet. And so between
my endeavors to qualify for passing the preliminary
examination of the Royal College of Surgeons, I began
to write; I should think the most horrible drivel that
ever has been written since rhymes first jingled. I can't
remember, oddly enough, whether I tried to imitate
Swinburne; I know one copy of verses was "inspired"
by a picture called "Harmony," which I think was hung
in the Academy of 1880. It depicted a mediæval maiden
playing the organ, while a mediæval youth watched her
in a dazed and love-stricken condition. This is positively the only one of these early horrors of mine, of
which I have any recollection; my memory is purged

of the rest of them, I am glad to say. I merely mention these things because they illustrate a very singular point in literary psychology; in universal psychology, for the matter of that. For I believe it is a rule that almost every literary career, certainly every literary career which is to be concerned with the imaginative side of literature, begins with the writing of verses. Nay, people who are to live lives quite remote from literature will often try to write poetry in their youth; and on the face of it, this is a great puzzle. For poetry, be it remembered, is the most "artificial" kind of literary composition, it is immeasurably the most difficult, it is by far the most remote from that which is commonly called life. Why, then, does the inexperienced beginner, devoid of all technical ability, invariably essay this most difficult technical task on his entry into the literary career?

The problem of the boy in the back room, not far from the dark stream of the Wandle, writing verses in the red notebook, is really one of the enigmas of the universe; it is rather a Chinese-box puzzle; riddle is within riddle.

For if we start at the beginning of things, or at what seems to us to be the beginning of things, we are met by the question as to why there should be any such thing as poetry in the universe. I need not say how much wider this question is than it seems; how it must be asked about all the arts, about fugues and cathedrals and romances and dances. It is an immense question; immense when one considers that with nine people out of ten the great criterion is, "Does it pay?" That is, will it result in a larger supply of fine champagne, four ale, roast legs of pork, and mousses royales to the population? Will this scheme of things enable Sir John to keep a fifth motorcar, or will it get Bill meat three times a day? That is, at last, the test by which we judge

all things. It is an old and approved British test; by it
Macaulay condemned the whole of Greek philosophy,
because that philosophy did not lead up to the inven-
tion of the steam engine. Now, it is quite clear that
poetry, speaking generally, pays neither the producer
nor the consumer of it; it does not lead to motorcars,
beefsteaks, vintage clarets, or four ale. It is not even
moral; not a single man has ever been induced to drink
ginger-beer instead of beer by reading Keats.

I must pause for a moment; I fear that it may be
thought that I am trying to be funny or — more
injurious accusation! — trying to be clever. I am not
trying to be either; I am stating the simple facts of the
case. Hardly a month passes by without some indig-
nant person pointing out in the Press that Engineering
and Commercial Chemistry are infinitely more useful
— i.e., lead to more beefsteaks — than Latin and Greek;
and that when Oxford and Cambridge find out that
obvious truth they may become of some service to the
State. Indeed, it is only a few weeks ago since a gentleman wrote to a paper showing that military training
was better for a boy — i.e., would make him the better
soldier — than "silly old" Greek plays. And let me
acknowledge that these contentions are perfectly true;
just as it is perfectly true that fur coats are much
warmer than Alcaics. So, I say, here is the problem: the
common, widely accepted test of the right to existence
of everything: does it pay, does it add to the physical
comforts of life, is quite clearly opposed to the existence of poetry, and yet poetry exists. Therefore, either
the poets and the lovers of poetry are mad, or else the
common judgment is . . . let us say, mistaken. I need
scarcely say that I incline to the latter solution of the
problem, and so qua human being, I am not ashamed
of trying to write poetry by the Wandle, though I

recognize, qua Arthur Machen, that I was, very decidedly, not born a poet.

For I firmly hold the doctrine that the natural, the
arch-natural expression of man, so far as he is to be
distinguished from pigs and dogs and goats, is in the
arts, and through the arts and by the arts. It is not by
reason, as reason is commonly understood, that man
is distinguished from the other animals; but by art. I
can quite well conceive the Black Ants sending the
message "Hill 27 fell before the Red Ant attack early
this afternoon," but I cannot conceive either Red or
Black Ants writing odes or building miniature cathedrals. The arts, then, are man's difference, that which
makes him to be what he is; and when he speaks
through them he is using the utterance which is proper
to him, as man. For, if we once set aside the "does it
pay" nonsense, which is evidently nonsense and pesti-
lent nonsense at that, we come clearly and freely to the
truth that man is concerned with beauty, and with the
ecstasy or rapture that proceeds from the creation of
beauty and from the contemplation of it. And youth,
as I think I have pointed out before, is the time of
revelation. It is children who possess the "kingdom of
heaven," to them are vouchsafed glimpses of that paradise which is the true home of man, and so it is that
the boy with literature in his blood naturally makes
his first efforts in the region of poetry, which is the
heart and core of all literature.

The heart and core; for, as in the individual man, so
in the whole history of men literature begins always
with poetry, just as speech began with song. First, the
magic incantation, sung about strange secret fires in
hidden places by wild men, then the ballad or lyric,
then Homer, then Herodotus, with the odors of the
sanctuary of poetry still about him, though he has
come down into the marketplace of prose. And it is

not necessary to go farther in time or space than the Northumberland of a few years ago to hear phrases common enough, things of everyday, set to enchanting melodies. I shall never forget how once in the years of my wandering I came one wet autumn afternoon to a little town called Morpeth. It struck me as a dingy place enough, "un petit trou de province, sale, noir, boueux," and my lodging was dingy, and musty too, in a house kept by an old invalid woman who moved about in a wheel chair and grumbled if a window were opened. But when it came to the question of the stroller's tea, the servant-maid, who came, I think, from the wild places of that land, said consolingly: "You need not trouble yourselves; you shall have your tea in half an hour." No doubt the girl was mortal, but she spoke the tongue of the immortals; her phrase about our tea was chanted to an exquisite melody that might have come from the Gradual — or from fairyland.

The natural man, then, is a singer and a poet, and so we may say that all artists are in reality survivals from an earlier time, and so it is that even in these later days the lad, with something of the youth and true nature of his race restored to him for a brief hour, sits in solitary places and endeavors to exercise his birth-right. Alas! he stutters deplorably in his speech as he delays by the Wandle, inditing verses; but it is thus that he would declare that he is a citizen of no mean city; he would fain say through those sorry rhymes, *Civis coelestis sum.*

Chapter IV

*W*ell, I saw the first of Augustus Harris's autumn dramas at Drury Lane, heard the newsboys calling out the death of Miss Neilson one misty evening up and down the Strand, and went back to Gwent in the character of a bad penny; and so fell to writing of those autumn and winter nights, when all the house was still.

Poor wretch! For this is the misery of literature, that it has no technique in the sense that music and painting have each its own technique. The young painter and the young composer, having acquired a certain mechanical skill in the elements of their arts, have studios and schools which they can attend. They have masters who lead them in their several ways, or who tell them, if necessary, to abandon those ways with all convenient speed. But for the lad with letters on the brain there is no help, no guidance; nor is there the possibility of any direction in the literary path. Now and then people send me manuscripts, and ask for my opinion; I give it because I am weak, but I always tell them that in literature the other man's opinion is not worth twopence.

No; the only course is to go on stumbling and struggling and blundering like a man lost in a dense thicket on a dark night; a thicket, I say, of rebounding boughs that punish with the sting of a whip-lash, of thorns that most savagely lacerate the flesh — it is the flesh of the heart, alas! that they tear — of sharp rocks of agony and black pools of despair. Such is the obscure wood of the literary life; such, at least, it was to me. You struggle to find your way; but again and again you ask yourself whether, for you, there is any way. You think you have hit upon the lucky track at last. And lo! before your feet is the black pit. And such is not alone the adventure of little, ineffectual, struggling men. How old was glorious Cervantes, now serene forever amongst the immortals, when he found his way to that village of La Mancha? Fifty, I think, or almost fifty. And he had been striving for years to write plays, and poetry, and short stories of passion and sentiment; and it was only the roar of applause that thundered up from the world when the Knight and the Squire were seen riding over the hill that convinced Cervantes that at last he had discovered his true path; if indeed he ever were convinced in his heart of the magnitude and majesty of the achievement of "Don Quixote."

And if these things are done with the great, what will be done with the little? If the clear-voiced rulers of the everlasting choir are to suffer so and agonize, what of miserable little Welshmen stammering and stuttering by the Wandle, in the obscure rectory amongst the hills, in waste places by Shepherd's Bush, in gloomy Great Russell Street, where the ghosts of dead, disappointed authors go sighing to and fro? For the fate of the little literary man there is no articulate speech that is sufficient; one must fall back on aoi or oimoi, or alas, or some such vague lament of unutterable woe.

Now one of the first agonies of the learner in letters is the discovery of the horrid gulf that yawns between the conception and the execution. Some years before

this winter of 1880, when I was at school, I had read
the tale of Owain in the Mabinogion, of the magic
sudden storm, and of the singing of the birds after it.
And going out for a walk one half-holiday with a
school-fellow, just such a sudden storm, as it seemed
to me, overtook us as we went down into a beautiful
valley not far from Hereford; and after it there was a
like joyful singing of birds in the trees. And somehow
the magic atmosphere of the old tale, mingled with the
enacting, as it were, of one of its chief circumstances,
left on my mind a very strong and singular impression
which, when the desire of literature came upon me, I
yearned to put into words. I did so, in the blank verse
form, and sent the "poem" to the "Gentleman's Magazine," and this I think was my first attempt to get into
print. I need not say that my nonsense was returned to
me, with thanks; but I wish I knew why I chose that
particular magazine. It must have had some especial
attraction for me, since ten years later I sent Sylvanus
Urban a prose article, which he accepted and paid for
at the appropriate eighteenth-century rate of a guinea
a sheet; that is sixteen pages. But I must say in all
fairness that Sylvanus warned me in advance of his rate
of payment.

But that gulf between the idea as it glows warm and
radiant in the author's heart, and its cold and faulty
realization in words is an early nightmare, and a late
one, too. For the beginner, if he suffer from many
terrible disappointments, has also the consolations of
hope, fallacious though these may prove to be. This
scheme that looked so well has certainly come to the
saddest grief, but there may be better luck next time;
if this road have led to nothing but a blank wall of
failure, that way may rise from the valley and climb
the hill and lead into a fair land. It is later in the life
of the literary man, when he has tried all roads and

made all the experiments, that his final sorrow comes upon him. He may not be forced to say, perhaps, that he has been a total failure; he may, indeed, be able to chronicle achievements of a minor kind, successes in the estimation of others. But now, with riper understanding, he perceives, as he did not perceive in the days of his youth, the depth of the gulf between the idea and the word, between the emotion that thrilled him to his very heart and soul, and the sorry page of print into which that emotion stands translated. He dreamed in fire; he has worked in clay.

I did not know (happily for myself) of these things in the ending of the year 1880; and so, when all the rectory was abed and asleep, I sat up by a dying fire writing a "poem" on a classic subject.

The classic "poem" was finished some time in the winter of 1880–81, and then I performed a bold action. I sent the manuscript — I can see it now, written in a sprawly hand on both sides of ordinary letter paper — to a Hereford stationer, and bade him print me one hundred copies thereof. He, strangely enough, did so, and I saw myself in print for the first time. I have been looking at my copy of this work, I should think the only copy in existence, and wondering whether I would quote a few lines from it. I have decided against this course. But, after all, I was only seventeen when I wrote "Eleusinia."

But the little pamphlet had its influence on my life. My relations decided, after reading it, that journalism was the career for me; a decision that then seemed to me both reasonable and pleasant, which now strikes me with amazement, nay with stupefaction. Since those days I have found out a good many things concerning both poetry and journalism; and looking over that old copy of "Eleusinia," I have meditated on what career I should advise for the author of that work if he were now to consult me. I give it up; I abandon the problem utterly. And yet, strange as it seems, strange most of all to me, my relations were justified after all. I did become a journalist, just thirty years afterwards. But by 1910, those who had arranged this destiny for me were long dead and delivered from all their troubles. I remember my father, who knew about as much of the matter as I did, sketching out my future career. I was to go to London to learn the business first of all, shorthand, of course, and all that sort of thing. A chief portion of the task, he said, half jocularly, would be to lurk in the entrance-halls of great houses and write down the names of distinguished guests on the nights of grand receptions. And then, eventually, some few hundreds would come to me, and with this I was to buy an interest in a small local paper, and so, I suppose, write leaders and live happily ever after. The program has not been carried out literally. The few hundreds have been more agreeably spent long years ago, and my editor never sent me to get the names of distinguished guests at great houses — knowing, wise man, that I should make a sad mess of such a business. But one of my first "assignments" in journalism was to describe a Giant Apple. I chased after that apple from Bond Street to Covent Garden, from Covent Garden back to Bond Street, and wrote in my paper about its smiling face, wishing my poor father were alive to hear the story of my long-deferred entrance into the art and mystery of the journalist. He would have laughed consumedly; and from my dear remembrance of him, I think he would have found a quotation from Horace to meet the case. Once, I recollect, it turned out that the odd man at the rectory, supposed to be a bachelor, had abandoned a wife and twelve children — all of them small ones, for aught I know — somewhere in Gloucestershire. A policeman came for poor Robert, and my father was very sorry for the man, even though he were a sad dog, and a notorious toper of ale. But the rector thought of the phrase: "Raro antecedentem scelestum deseruit poena," and cheered up amazingly.

Well, on the strength of the verses about the Eleusinian mysteries, I am to be a journalist, and consequently, as it was thought in those days, I must learn shorthand, so that I may be able to write a hundred and fifty words in a minute. And here again comes a chapter as sad as that which I have written on my arithmetic. I never learnt shorthand effectively, because I was too stupid to learn it. The queer thing is that when I was quite a little boy at school this art of shorthand had a strange and mysterious attraction for me. Why? I am sure I don't know; why did the small boys of my generation love dark lanterns? Robert Louis Stevenson has written an enchanting essay on the fascination of this instrument of the mysteries; but I am not quite sure that even he has penetrated to the heart of the enigma. For I, though a lonely child, knew the joy of the dark lantern, and it was a great and exceeding joy. The glowing of heat that rose from its roof — corrugated, I think? — the rank smell of its oils were charms that somehow carried me over the borders of this common world into an exquisite region of wonder and surmise. And now I come to look back into days horribly distant — the shorthand question must wait for a while — I perceive that there was a perfect ritual, or ceremonial rather, of the Dark Lantern, the origins of which are as obscure to me as are the origins of other primitive mysteries. Of one thing only I am certain, and I speak with all due deference to the author of "The Golden Bough," not forgetting Miss Jane Harrison; the lantern service of my early boyhood had no reference whatever to the young crops or to the sprouting of the corn. As I lit the wick I did not say, "O Sun! shine thou also on the land and make it warm so that there may be many cabbages, so that green peas may not be lacking to the lamb which is equally nurtured by thy beams." Of course, I am quite willing to allow that, as a general rule, an anxiety about the spring crops fully explains the origin of all painting, all sculpture, all architecture, all poetry, all drama, all music, all religion, all romance: I admit that the Holy Gospels are really all about spring cabbage, that martyrdom and mass are spring cabbage, that Arthur is really arator, the plowman; that Galahad, denoting the achievement and end of the great quest, is Caulahad, the cabbage god. I admit all this because it is so entirely reasonable and satisfactory, and, indeed, self-evident; but though all Frazerdom should rise up against me, I cannot allow that when I lit my dark lantern I was inviting the sun to help the crops.

There was some sort of obscure connection — I seem to remember — between Dark Lanterns and Masks. They were both properties in singular mysteries of a formless character which were enacted in dark shrubberies on dark nights, just before bedtime. It was well understood, I know, that these objects must be kept in secret places, and must not by any means be seen by the uninitiated; and the uninitiated were everybody besides myself. And here, I believe, I was following unconsciously, but most strictly, the rules of all primitive mysteries throughout the world. The Greeks of the historical period had become lax; they carried about the mystic fan of Iacchus in public procession. But amongst the Blackfellows of Australia, where the rites are much nearer to the original purity of their institution, the mystic fan is not seen, only heard. Therefore the Dark Lantern and the Mask were kept hidden in an obscure cranny of the coach-house, which was at the end of an overshadowed drive at some distance from the rectory. They were produced under the cover of the darkness, these sacramental instruments, clouds and stars and the dim boughs of trees and tangled undergrowth alone saw them. There were certain solemn words which accompanied the ostension of the objects, but they were in a language which I have long forgotten. But some day, when the turmoil has died down, when the clouds have cleared for the sunset and the apparition of the evening star, as I sit by a western shore awaiting the boat of Avalon, I shall write my last treatise, under the title of "The Dark Lantern and the Mask," *libellus vere mysticus*. And here I give notice to all good and lawful men that I am duly seized of the above title, so that they may abstain from intromitting with the same.

This digression of the dark lantern proceeded, naturally enough, from my speaking of shorthand. This art, I said, appealed to me when I was a boy, and its appeal was that of a kind of mystery writing, of a script not in common use. For my acquaintance did not lie in journalistic circles. I knew nobody who could write shorthand or understood anything about it, and so the three books of Pitman — "Teacher," "Manual," and "Reporter" — were three mystery books, so far as my small world was concerned. But now, in later years, having written that famous poem on the initiation of Eleusis, I was to be a journalist, and to be a journalist I must learn shorthand. And then I found Phonography a mystery indeed, and too great a mystery for me, since I could not attain to it. I muddled about with it for three or four years; I actually made some use of it in one of my queer employments, but I never wrote it decently. I was too fumble-fisted; try as I would, I could not form the characters with elegance or accuracy. My p's and b's would wobble and bend till they looked

like f's and v's, if I tried to halve a letter I quartered it.
A kindly reporter gave me a hint: "Don't bother about
the thick and thin lines," he said, "I never do." And
no doubt the skilled shorthand writer can play all
manner of tricks with the system, but I was not a skilled
writer, and I took the reporter's advice and made bad
worse. My last shorthand lesson was taken in 1885,
long after I had ceased to think of journalism as a
profession. Indeed, I cannot now remember why I
continued to waste my time over a craft that I could
not master; but I suppose I thought the endeavor gave
an air of respectability and solidity to my proceedings
that they would have lacked without it. From June 1881
to December 1882 I was more or less vaguely bent on
the journalist's career. I remember feeling somewhat
discouraged during this period by reading an advertisement for a journalistic position in a London paper.
The applicant could write shorthand at the rate of one
hundred and fifty words a minute, he understood all
about reporting, he was an expert at "leaderettes," and
quite willing to take a turn at the case — all for thirty
shillings a week. This did not seem promising, but I
need not have disturbed myself; my journalistic days
were not yet, nor for many years to come. In the
meanwhile I read variously and became thoroughly
familiar with Boswell's Johnson (in Mr. Percy Fitzger-
ald's edition). And one windy, gusty night, when the
costers' flares in the back streets were burning with a
rushing sound, I came upon a secondhand bookshop
on the main road between Hammersmith and Turnham Green, and went in and found an odd volume of
William Morris's "Earthly Paradise." Now followed
the old trouble, and in a worse form. As Swinburne's
"Songs Before Sunrise" had first set me versifying, so
the "Earthly Paradise" reinforced the original virus.
And now I had acquired some slight facility of a

worthless sort, and so I began to imitate William Morris, and spent the odd hours of six good months in writing a sham-Greek tale in rhymed couplets; which I tore up thirty years ago. And then I discovered Herrick, and tried to imitate that inimitable writer; but this effort, though vain in itself, was not so wholly vain. For it brought me, as it were, into the seventeenth century, into an age which I have loved ever since with a peculiar devotion. Ten years later I went on pilgrimage to Dean Prior and Dean Churchtown, and in spite of the restored church, trod the lanes under the moor with reverence, since Herrick's feet had passed by those ways.

But now towards the end of the year 1882, after I had known London, on and off, for nearly two and a half years, all that feeling of its immense gaiety with which I had approached it in the first place was dropping from me. I began to realize, very gradually and by dismal degrees, that the gaieties of London were commodities that had to be bought with money, and that I had none. The theater had ceased to charm me, and I am very sorry to say that it has never charmed me since; that is from the point of view of the man sitting in the pit. By the end of '82 I had quite definitely ceased to be "fond of the play."

For now London began to assume for me its terrible aspect. It was rather a goblin's castle than a city of delights; if indeed it had not become a place of punishment wherein I was condemned to hard labor through many dreary and hopeless years.

Chapter V

*I*n that wonderful volume which is called the Grand
Saint Graal we are told how the hermit Nasciens received a magic book from paradise. It was divided into
portions, and one of these portions was intituled "Here
Begin Terrors." I can find no words that might more
fitly introduce the tale of my solitary life in London.
I was only twenty; I was poor; I was desolate. And I
frizzled all the time (or most of it) on the fire of my
own futility; I longed to make literature, and I could
only write nonsense.

I was employed for a time in a house of business in
a street north of the Strand and parallel to it, which, I
suppose, must have been Chandos Street. I know that
it was still paved with cobble-stones. My employers
were publishers — the firm has for many years ceased
to exist — and I was something or other in what is called
the "editorial" department. But to the best of my belief
publishing books was but a minor part of the energies
of the house, and I should think a later growth. The
real staple was wholesale stationery; there was an important "line" of copybooks, there was a great deal
done with ornamental and decorated albums, and also
with pictorial calendars. The Shakespeare calendar of

the House is still in existence, or was in existence a year or two ago, and it bears the name of the vanished firm. Mr. (afterwards Sir) Walter Besant had been the "editor" of Messrs. Chandos and Co., but just before I made my first trial of business life he had resigned, and his place was taken by a very kindly literary gentleman, whose name I have forgotten. Afterwards he edited a series, if not several series, of anthologies, and was, I believe, appointed Professor of English Literature at some Indian seminary of learning. I do not know whether he is still alive. Well, it was my business to assist this gentleman. I think I was engaged as his "secretary," but I was known in the House as his "clurk." I am trying to recollect what I actually did to assist him.

My first job on the morning of my arrival I can remember. I made a copy of Mr. Gladstone's Latin version of the well-known hymn, "Rock of Ages": "Jesu, pro me perforatus," it began. And then I had to take down in shorthand and afterwards write in longhand a stern letter to somebody who had made a mistake in the name of King Alfred's grandmother. This error had occurred in one of a series of Board School history books that the firm was publishing; and this circumstance alone gave me a loathing and hatred for the whole business, since I thought then, and think still, that the name of King Alfred's grandmother is not of the faintest consequence to any reasonable being. It is the kind of fact which would interest a German deeply; he would spend years of his life to find out all about it; but such is not the occupation of a gentleman.

In the afternoon of that day we became a little livelier. My chief contributed a London letter to some Scottish paper — he came from the northern part of this island — and again my shorthand was required.

The London letter was distinctly gay in its tone, it dealt in a cheerful spirit with some early incidents in the career of a certain admirable actress whose talents then engaged and delighted us. As I took it down it struck me as over worldly for the readers of the "Haddaneuk Herald," and sure enough my man reconsidered the matter and struck out the gaieties from the copy. And how did that famous shorthand of mine serve me? Not so vilely, considering all things. I had a quick memory then, and remembered many of the phrases that had been dictated, and I could read quite a lot of the characters that I had formed, and others gave me a vague sort of intimation of the sense; just as the neumes helped the church-singers of the earlier ages; they were quite useful if you knew the tune.

I search my memory for further details of my occupation with Chandos and Co. I think that the Shakespeare Calendar occupied me during odd hours for a week or more. This was January, and I was set to the preparation of the calendar for the next year. It was not a difficult task, and I was furnished with a sort of album, containing the Shakespeare calendars for the past six or seven years, and my only business was to make a new almanack out of these old elements. Thus January 1, 1884, gave the Shakespearean quotation that had been assigned to December 27, 1877; for January 2 I chose a motto that had pertained to February 6, 1882, and so forth. It was easy, but dull. And I was dull, too, or I would have invented Shakespearean lines that Shakespeare never wrote, and trusted to the all but universal ignorance of Shakespeare. I did something like that, when I was an older and a merrier man. I persuaded a friend of mine, a young fellow of literary tastes, that one of the most famous phrases ascribed to Shakespeare was in reality a gag, invented by Mr. F. R. Benson's stage manager. "Do you mean to say," said my friend, "that this Mr. Randle Ayrton invented 'a poor thing, but mine own'?" "Certainly," I replied. "Then," said he, "Ayrton must be a most wonderful man." And I wonder how many of my readers know exactly how the matter stands — without referring to the play?

And then what else did I do for my pound a week in Chandos Street? Chiefly, I think I took down and transcribed a daily report to the head office of the firm, which was in Belfast or Dundee or some such town. I don't remember in the least what it was about, whether it dealt with King Alfred's grandmother's name or with other matters. But I had to write about two quarto pages daily of this report, and put D 1 in the margin. I think D 1 meant Literary Department; but the whole thing was the terror of my life. For it had to be neatly written, with a fair and level margin on each side; and this I could by no means achieve. Again and again my D 1 was condemned as a ragged and untidy perform-ance, and I had to copy it out all over again, as if I had been a careless schoolboy — as, indeed, I was from the firm's point of view.

And I sit in my corner, trying to write a round, clear, clerkly hand, trying to remember that of the two forms of the small "t" one was much to be preferred, trying to observe the rule that "today" must be written as one word, not two, and that for commercial purposes "draft" must be spelt with "f," not with "ugh"; and thinking of the nightingale in the thorn bush by the Soar, in the still valley.

Here I was, then, in Chandos Street, a peg of no particular shape at all in a perfectly round hole, feeling very miserable indeed. We were, I believe, somewhat cramped for room, and I had a desk in the album department. Here three very cheerful and kindly young fellows of about my own age did something with handsome albums. I don't know in the least what they did; so far as I could see they took albums out of tissue paper and put them back into tissue paper all day long. One of them, the senior of the room — he must have been three or four years older than any of us — was just about to make a real start in life. He used to tell me all about it when we were alone together for a minute or two, as sometimes happened. There was a young lady whom he was to marry in a few months' time, and he had made arrangements for setting up as a stationer in Harlesden, and he meant to push Chandos's stuff — albums and everything — and to do well and be happy. "Poor man, and then he died," to quote one of Dr. Johnson's muttered undertones. I do not know how far his short life at Harlesden was successful or felicitous. But as for me, I hated it all. It was not that the work was hard, but that I took no interest in it, and saw no reason why it should be done at all, or why anybody alive should do it. So I looked about me, and through the favor of a friend I got a little teaching of small children at twenty-five shillings a week. Then I gave notice to Messrs. Chandos. They were very kind; they offered me twenty-five shillings a week to stay, but I thanked them and said no. It was the business atmosphere of the place that I detested; I have always agreed with the small boy in "Nicholas Nickleby" who uttered the great maxim, "Never Perform Business." The teaching which followed was certainly not exciting, but I did not mind it. Indeed, having to teach Euclid, I found to my amazement that it was about something, and actually was a coherent and reasoned scheme of things, not a mere madhouse puzzle, as I had always imagined. But then my own geometrical instruction had been limited. It consisted simply in this: Fourteen Euclids were served out to fourteen small boys. The mathematical master then said: "Learn the Definitions,

Axioms, and Postulates." That was my first and my last lesson in geometry; though I duly went through the accustomed books of Euclid, trying to learn by heart what was to me mere unmeaning gibberish.

At this time and for the next year and a half I was living in Clarendon Road, Notting Hill Gate — or Holland Park, to give the politer subdirection. I am sorry to say that I had not a garret, since the houses of that quarter, being comparatively modern, do not possess the sloping roofs which have seen the miseries of so many lettered men. Still, my room had its merits. It was, of course, at the top of the house, and it was much smaller than any monastic "cell" that I have ever seen. From recollection I should estimate its dimensions as ten feet by five. It held a bed, a washstand, a small table, and one chair; and so it was very fortunate that I had few visitors. Outside, on the landing, I kept my big wooden box with all my possessions — and these not many — in it. And there was a very notable circumstance about this landing. On the wall was suspended, lengthwise, a step-ladder by which one could climb through a trapdoor to the roof in case of fire, and so between the rungs or steps of this ladder I disposed my library. For anything I know, the books tasted as well thus housed as they did at a later period when I kept them in an eighteenth-century bookcase of noble dark mahogany, behind glass doors. There was no fireplace in my room, and I was often very cold. I would sit in my shabby old great-coat, reading or writing, and if I were writing I would every now and then stand up and warm my hands over the gas-jet, to prevent my fingers getting numb. I remember envying a man very much indeed on a certain night in late winter or early spring. It was a very cold night; there was a bitter northeaster blowing, and the wind seemed to pierce right through my old coat and to set my very bones shivering and aching. I had gone abroad, because I was weary of my den, because I was sick with reading and in no humor for writing, because I felt I must have some change, however slight. But it was an evil and a bitter blast, so I turned back after a little while, coming down one of the steep streets that lead from Notting Hill Gate Station to Clarendon Road. And halfway home I came upon a man encamped on the road by the pavement. He was watching over some barrows and tools and other instruments of street repair, and he sat in a sort of canvas wigwam, well sheltered from the wind that was chilling me to the heart. His coat, too, looked thick and heavy, and he had a warm comforter round his neck, and before him was a glowing, ardent brazier of red-hot coals. He held his hands and his nose over the radiant heat, and smoked a black clay pipe; and I think he had a can of beer beside him. I envied that man with all my heart; I don't think I have ever envied any man so much.

Occasionally I had applications for the loan of a book from my step-ladder library. These came from the lodgers on the ground floor, an Armenian and his wife, who annoyed the landlady by sleeping in cushions piled about the carpet and hanging their blankets in front of the doors and windows. It was the Armenian lady who had literary tastes, and her desire was always for "a story-book." I never saw her or her husband, but I often heard him calling Mary, the servant. He would stand at the top of the kitchen stairs and shout "Marry! Marry!" and then, reflectively, and after a short interval, "Damn that girl." He gave a fine, Oriental force to the common English "damn." Other lodgers that I remember were a young Greek and a chorus girl, mates for a single summer. They occupied the first floor and were succeeded by a family from Ireland. I have a confused notion that there was something a little queer

about the head of this household. He was, I think, a
major, and I know he was Evangelical. As I went down
the stairs I heard him more than once uttering in loud,
earnest tones the words, "Let us pray." This was startling; and one of his daughters would always shut the
door of their room with a bang on these occasions,
and that was startling, too.

The little table in my little room turned out to be a
very useful piece of furniture. I not only read at it and
wrote on it, but I used it as a larder. In the corner
nearest the angle of the wall by the window I kept my
provisions, that is to say, a loaf of bread and a canister
of green tea. Morning and evening the landlady or
"Marry" would bring me up a tray on which were a
plate, a knife, a teapot, a cup and saucer, and a jug of
hot water. With the aid of a kettle and a spirit lamp,
which came, I think, from under that serviceable table
— one may fairly say from the cellar — I made the hot
water to boil and brewed a great pot of strong green
tea.

In the first months of this life of mine an early
dinner was added to the fees of my teaching; later, my
pupils changed, and the dinner disappeared. I then
used to spend the hour in the middle of the day in
wanderings about Turnham Green and the waste places
round Gunnersbury, making my meal on a large Cap-
tain's biscuit and a glass of beer. I varied this repast by
taking it in various public-houses. In those days there
were still pleasing and ancient taverns scattered along
those western roads. One I remember in particular, a
very old, tumbledown house, set at the edge of the
market gardens, which then approached almost to
Turnham Green. There was not a straight line about
this old, old house, its roof tree dipped and wavered,
and the roof was of mellowed tiles, and one end of the
place was quite overwhelmed by a huge billow of ivy.

I used to think that highwaymen must have lurked in the little room where I took my biscuit and glass of ale; and the food and drink tasted much better on that account. The old tavern, and its leaning sheds and ragged outbuildings, its red roof and its green ivy; all are gone long ago. There is a row of raw houses where it stood, and I hate them. Sometimes I did not have any beer, either because I did not want any, or because it struck me as too great a luxury. Then I would buy a small bag of currant biscuits and take them to the region of the market gardens and devour them, sitting on a gate or sheltering behind a hedge. I don't know how it is, but these feasts are always connected in my mind with a grey and gloomy sky and a very cold wind, so that I shiver when I think of flat, square biscuits in which currants are embedded. But I have a reverence for them, too. There were, I confess, days of gross debauch. Once a week, or once a fortnight at the least, I went to a goodly and spacious and ancient tavern on the high road, and had a grilled chop, potatoes, bread, and beer; which came to one and a penny or one and twopence. *Les Côtelettes de Mouton, Sauce Bénie* the dish is called by the experts of the *haute cuisine.* I can recommend it. And in the evenings I sometimes exceeded, though not so violently. I would, nine evenings out of ten, buy my provision of bread at a shop at the bottom of the long main road, opposite or nearly opposite to Uxbridge Road Station. The shop kept a very choice kind of gingerbread, and I would buy a couple of bricks of this gingerbread, and munch them with a high relish as a supplement to the common bread.

As the spring of 1883 advanced, and the weather improved and the evenings lengthened, I began the habit of rambling abroad in the hope of finding something that could be called country. I would sometimes pursue Clarendon Road northward and get into all sorts of regions of which I never had any clear notion. They are obscure to me now, and a sort of nightmare. I see myself getting terribly entangled with a canal which seemed to cross my path in a manner contrary to the laws of reason. I turn a corner and am confronted with an awful cemetery, a terrible city of white gravestones and shattered marble pillars and granite urns, and every sort of horrid heathenry. This, I suppose, must have been Kensal Green: it added new terror to death. I think I came upon Kensal Green again and again; it was like the Malay, an enemy for months. I would break off by way of Portobello Road and entangle myself in Notting Hill, and presently I would come upon the goblin city; I might wander into the Harrow Road, but at last the ghost-stones would appall me. Maida Vale was treacherous, Paddington false — inevitably, it seemed, my path led me to the detested habitation of the dead.

Be it remembered that my horror at the sight of Kensal Green Cemetery was due to this, that, odd as it may seem to townsfolk, I had never seen a cemetery before. Well I knew the old graveyards of Gwent, solemn amongst the swelling hills, peaceful in the shadow of very ancient yews. I knew well these garths. There was Henllis, high up on the mountain side, in the place of roaring winds, under the færy dome of Twyn Barlwm. I had lingered there of autumn evenings while the sun set red over the mountains, and a drift of rain came with the gathering darkness, as the yew boughs beat upon the east window of the church. There were graves there with flourished inscriptions, deeply cut, and queer Welsh rhymes — *dyma gareg dêg:* —

Here's a rare stone — of death.
Beneath it lies
A rarer dust, that shall arise

By heavenly breath alone; and climb the skies —
We trust.

I knew the churchyard of Llanddewi, looking down
the steep hillside into the chanting valley of the Soar,
and Kemeys, between the Forest and the Usk, and
Partrishw, in the heart of the wild mountains beyond
Abergavenny. These places of the dead were solemn
with old religion, and the tones of *Dirige* and *De
Profundis* and *Requiem Æternam* sang still about them
on their hills; but this white ghostly city of corruption
— there was nothing but horror in it! Still, I see myself
on these wanderings, beating to and fro in the stony
wilderness, entangled, as I say, in the endless mazes of
unknown streets. Now I would succeed in breaking
away. I would pass that sad zone of destruction and
disgrace that always lies just beyond the furthest points
of the suburb. These are the places where the hedges
are half ruined, half remaining, where the little winding brook is defiled, but not yet a drain, where one tree
lies felled and withered, while its fellow is still all green.
Here curbstones impinge on the fields, and show where
new, rabid streets are to rush up the sweet hillside and
capture it; here the well under the thorn is choked with
a cartload of cheap bricks lately deposited. I would pass
over these dismal regions and come, as I thought, into
the fair open country, and then suddenly at the turn
of the lane I would be confronted by red ranks of
brand-new villas: this might be Harlesden or the out-
posts of Willesden.

I think that on the especial occasion that I have in
mind the red row of houses must have been some
portion or fragment of Harlesden. I remember that,
like the cemetery, this impressed me as a wholly new

and unforeseen horror, something as strange and terrible as the apparition of a rattlesnake or a boa-constrictor might be to an English child, wandering a little away into the orchard or the wood near the house. I had never lived in a world that might have prepared me for such things; in Gwent — in my day, at all events — there was no such phenomenon as this sudden and violent irruption of red brick in the midst of a green field; and thus when I came round the corner of a peaceful lane and saw in the midst of elms and meadows this staring spectacle, I was as aghast as Robinson Crusoe when he saw the track of the foot on the sand of his desert island.

. . . And here I would make a parenthesis, and say that so long as my writing habits had any concern with the imagination I never departed from the one formula. This not consciously; in fact, I have a secret doctrine to the effect that in literature no imaginative effects are achieved by logical predetermination. I have told, I think, how I was confronted suddenly and for the first time with the awe and solemnity and mystery of the valley of the Usk, and of the house called Bartholly hanging solitary between the deep forest and the winding esses of the river. This spectacle remained in my heart for years, and at last I transliterated it, clumsily enough, in the story of "The Great God Pan," which, as a friendly critic once said, "does at least make one believe in the devil, if it does nothing else." Here, of course, was my real failure; I translated awe, at worst awfulness, into evil; again, I say, one dreams in fire and works in clay. But, at all events, my method never altered. More legitimately than in the instance of "The Great God Pan" I made the horrid apparition of the crude new houses in the midst of green pastures the seed of my tale, "The Inmost Light," which was originally bound up with "The Great God Pan." And so the man in my story, resting in green fields, looked up and saw a face that chilled his blood gazing at him from the back of one of those red houses that once had frightened me, when I was a sorry lad of twenty, wandering about the verges of London. The doctor of my tale lived in Harlesden.

And if I may pursue this subject farther I would suggest that the whole matter of imaginative literature depends upon this faculty of seeing the universe, from the æonian pebble of the wayside to the raw suburban street as something new, unheard of, marvelous, finally, miraculous. The good people — amongst whom I naturally class myself — feel that everything is miraculous; they are continually amazed at the strangeness of the proportion of all things. The bad people, or scientists as they are sometimes called, maintain that nothing is properly an object of awe or wonder since everything can be explained. They are duly punished.

If we go more deeply into this text of Horror and Harlesden, it will become apparent, I think, that what is called genius is not only of many varying degrees of intensity, but also very distinctly of two parts or functions. There is the passive side of genius, that faculty which is amazed by the strange, mysterious, admirable spectacle of the world, which is enchanted and rapt out of our common airs by hints and omens of an adorable beauty everywhere latent beneath the veil of appearance. Now I think that every man or almost every man is born with the potentiality at all events of this function of genius. *Os homini sublime dedit, coelumque tueri*: man, as distinct from the other animals, carries his head on high so that he may look upon the heavens; and I think that we may say that this sentence has an interior as well as an exterior meaning. The beasts look downward, to the earth, not only in the letter but in the spirit; they are creatures of material sensation, living by far the greatest part of their lives in a world of hot and cold, hunger and thirst and satisfaction. Man, on the other hand, is by his nature designed to look upward, to gaze into the heavens that are all about him, to discern the eternal in things temporal. Or, as the Priestess of the Holy Bottle defines and distinguishes: the beasts are made to drink water, but men to drink wine. This, the receptive or passive part of genius, is, I say, given to every human being, at least potentially. We receive, each one of us, the magic bean, and if we will plant it it will undoubtedly grow and become our ladder to the stars and the cloud castles. Unfortunately the modern process, so oddly named civilization, is as killing to this kind of gardening as the canker to the rose; and thus it is that if I want a really nice chair, I must either buy a chair that is from a hundred to a hundred and fifty years old, or else a careful copy or replica of such a chair. It may appear strange to Tottenham Court Road and the modern furniture trade; but it is nonetheless true that you cannot design so much as a nice armchair unless you have gone a little way at all events up the magic beanstalk.

Still, many of us have our portion of the passive or perceptive faculty of genius; we are moved by the wonder of the world; we know ourselves as citizens of an incredible city, we catch stray glimpses of færy Atlantis, drowned beneath the ocean of sense. But it is one thing to dream dreams; and quite another to interpret them, and in this active faculty of interpretation, or translation of the heavenly tongues into earthly speech, there are infinite degrees of excellence. And the masters in this craft of interpretation are few indeed. And the final conclusion — a sad one for me — is that if I could have "translated" the Horror of

Harlesden competently I should have been a man of genius.

Still, I see myself all through that year 1883 tramping, loafing, strolling along interminable streets and roads lying to the northwest and the west of London, a shabby, sorry figure; and always alone. I remember walking to Hendon and back — this must have been on a whole holiday — and to this day I can't think how I found my way there, through what clues I struck from the north parts of Clarendon Road into the Harrow Road, and how I knew when to leave the Edgware Road and bend to the right. Anyhow, I got there and back, tired enough and glad of the half-loaf of bread that awaited me.

Then I became learned in Wormwood Scrubs and its possibilities. It was and is a very barren and bleak place itself, but in those days there was an attractive corner on the Acton side of the waste, that I was fond of contemplating. This was a sort of huddle of old cottages and barns and outhouses with a fringe of elms about them. It did my eyes good then as now to look on something that was old and worn with use and mellow; my eyes that were bleared and aching with the rawness and newness of multitudinous London. To me an old cottage, with its little latticed porch and its tangled garden patch, was veritable balm; I would gaze on such a place with refreshment and delight, as desert travelers must gaze on the cold pools and green leafage of an unexpected oasis. I used to light on these little, humble, pleasant retreats in my walks — there were many more of such cottages in the outskirts of London then than now — and make impossible plans for migrating from the urbanity of Clarendon Road into one

of these hidden places, where there would be a garden
for me to walk in, and perhaps a summer-house over-
grown with white roses, and a little low room with
oldish furniture. But I found no such place, and still
went prowling in a kind of torment of the spirit by the
highways and byways of the west. Acton used to do me
good; it was then more like a country town than a
modern suburb. On the right hand, as you came up
from the Uxbridge Road under the railway bridge,
there were then some grave and dignified houses of the
early Georgian period, with broad lawns before them
and big gardens behind them. On the left was the
Priory, with spacious and parklike grounds and many
greeny elms. Legends about the first Lord Lytton hung
about the Priory, and it was whispered that the old lady
who kept the lodge-gate had in her day written daring
poetry, of the erotic kind. There are laundries and rows
and rows of little houses now where the Priory stood;
the Georgian houses on the other side of the road have
all been pulled down. But I have a notion that the last
time I went that way I saw a second-hand bookshop
on the London side of the railway bridge, where in '83
I bought an old, odd volume of Cowley's poems.

The second-hand bookshop, which includes the
bookstall, is one of the many things that I have dabbled
in; but I have never been sworn to the hunt over the
old shelves as to a devouring passion. I lack the great
incentive: the love of rare books on account of their
rarity. I have a great respect for the collector of such
things, and I often envy him his sudden joys of discovery; it must be like finding a golden treasure in a
rubbish heap; but I could never follow his example.
Still, I often used to amuse myself by grubbing about
the dusty shelves for an odd hour or two, turning over
vast masses of insignificance — of insignificance for
me, at all events — conning titles, diving into prefaces,

glancing doubtfully over strange pages, wondering whether this or that or the other would bring me the best entertainment for the few shillings that I had to spend. In these new days the young man with a thirst for literature has his labors simplified; the classics of the world are ready for him, nicely printed, in a handy form, and at a low price. He has simply to go into a shop, put down his shilling, and get his book, and it is all over. This would never have done for me. When I bought a book I required and obtained a long drawn-out, deliberated pleasure; I considered that the possession of three-and-sixpence or five shillings entitled me to a whole afternoon's rich enjoyment. Just as ladies of the suburbs make arrangements — as I understand — to come up to town and do a little shopping, and have a delicate cress-sandwich or two in Regent Street, and then go to a matinée at the theater, and have creamy cakes for tea before they start back for the red villas: so did I use to travel from Notting Hill Gate to Charing Cross, and stroll up Villiers Street, and walk along the Strand, relishing its savors, which never grew stale to me. For I do believe that the old Strand, before they destroyed it with their porphyries and their marbles and Babylonian fooleries and façades of all sorts, was the very finest street in all the world. I know quite well its manifest and manifold weaknesses and faults, if it were to be regarded from the point of view of a classical town-architect. There was no plan, no design about it, no uniformity; its houses were of all shapes, sizes, periods, and heights; it had no more been designed than a wild hedgerow has been designed. And there, exactly, was its infinite and subtle and curious charm. Nothing could be more urban or urbane than the Strand; and yet it had grown, as the green brake grows, as the cathedrals and the country houses of England grew from age to age, gathering beauty as they increased. The Strand was an altogether English street, and it was the very heart of London. In it, or beside it, were the theaters and the bookshops and the cook-shops; to north and south odd passages and stairs and archways admitted the curious into the oddest places and quarters. You were weary of the traffic and the pattering feet? Then you could turn into New Inn or Clement's Inn and enjoy deep silence. You wanted to see the old hugger-mugger of the London back streets, dark taverns of the eighteenth century, where men had lain hidden from the hangman? Here was Clare Market for you. You had heard that "Elzevirs" were very rare and curious books, and would like to see an Elzevir? You would lose your opinion of their rarity, for you would see as many Elzevirs as any man could desire in Holywell Street, where I believe they were to be bought by the sack, as if they had been coals. And Elzevirs apart; the naughty prints and books of Holywell Street were as good as a play. For I believe that the Row had turned naughty somewhere in the early 'fifties; it had then got in its stocks — and had kept them. Here were the works of G. M. W. Reynolds in large volumes; "Mysteries of the Court of St. James," and such weari-ness. Here was the faded colored engraving of a young female of extreme gaiety — with ringlets, and the ap-pearance of the chambermaid in the once-famous print, "Sherry, sir." And with all the curiosity, and variety, and oddity and richness of the Strand, it had the while a manner of snug homeliness and coziness and comfort about it which was quite inimitable. To be in the Strand was like drinking punch and reading Dickens. One felt it was such a warmhearted, hospita-ble street, if one only had a little money. Unfortu-nately, I was never on dining terms, as it were, with the Strand; but I always felt that if it only knew me it would have called me "old boy" and given me its choicest saddles of mutton and its oldest port, and I felt grateful. Somehow I always warmed my hands when I got into the Strand . . . and they were often chilly enough.

Such, then, was my preparation for a book-foray in the heart of London, this relished, leisurely, savory walk along the Strand; and then I might dive into Clare Market by Clement's Inn and look for mystery books in a certain shop that I knew there. I bought one of the most curious — I do not say the best — books in the world, Vaughan's "Lumen de Lumine" in a shop in Clare Market, and still I should be much obliged if someone would tell me what "Lumen de Lumine" is about. Or I might try Denny's, at the western end of Booksellers' Row, or like enough go groveling round the shelves of Reeves and Turner, who were then in the southern bend of the Strand, opposite to St. Clement Dane's Church.

One dull afternoon, I remember, I ran to earth in this shop on a lower shelf a dim, brown elderly-looking book in cloth covers called "Ferrier's Institutes of Metaphysic." It repaid me many times over for the couple of shillings that I gave for it. I took Ferrier home in delight to the little room in Clarendon Road, and made a great deal of green tea, and found the dry bread of quite admirable flavor, and smoked pipes and read the new book far into the night. Before I went to bed Ferrier had quite convinced me of the truth of the proposition — which looked odd at first — that we can only be ignorant of that which we can know. This means, of course, that no man can be ignorant of the existence of four-sided triangles; which is evident enough. But as I fell asleep, I felt I had had a tremendous day.

I look back upon myself in that little room in Clarendon Road with some amazement. I come in from one of my long, prowling walks — I may have been to Hounslow to look for the Heath, or I may have been to Hampton Court — and make my meal of bread and tea, and then settle down to tobacco and literature. I find that my landlady turns off the gas at the meter at midnight, so I provide myself with carriage candles, which I fix up somehow on the table. I read on night after night. It may be Homer's "Odyssey," or it may be "Don Quixote" — to which I have been faithful ever since I found the book in the drawing room of Llanfrechfa Rectory — it may be that singular magazine of oddities, Disraeli's "Curiosities of Literature," it may be Burton's "Anatomy of Melancholy"; a great refuge, this last, a world of literature in itself. Or I am reading Pepys for the first time, with ravishment, or Pomponius Mela "De Situ Orbis" in a noble Stephanus quarto, or Harris's "Hermes," or Hargrave Jennings on the Rosicrucians; this last one of the craziest and most entertaining of books, which had a little later an odd influence on my fortunes. It was a sad blow to me to find out afterwards, chiefly through the medium of A. E. Waite's "Real History of the Rosicrucians," that, as a cold matter of fact, there were no Rosicrucians. A Lutheran pastor who had read Paracelsus, wrote, early in the seventeenth century, a pamphlet describing a secret order which had no existence outside of his brain. Naturally enough, societies arose which imitated, so far as they could, the imaginary organization described by the fantastic Johannes Valentinus Andrea; I should not be surprised, indeed, to be told that such societies are now in being in modern London; but these orders are late "fakes"; the 'seventies and 'eighties of the last century saw their beginnings. There are no Rosicrucians — and there never were any.

Or I am reading Carlyle — "Sartor Resartus" or the Johnson and Burns and Walter Scott Essays — and I must say that I think a good many young men of this age would be all the better for a Carlyle course. For though Carlyle was not the prophet of full inspiration that the time just before my own imagined, though he exalted brute force into a place that belongs to the Divine Wisdom, though his original Calvinism hung like a dark and obscuring cloud over all his life, yet I know not any man of these days that is worthy to dust Carlyle's hat or to clean his pipe for him.

There is a passage in the Johnson essay telling how the poor, agonized, heroic doctor made for himself a boat of the transient driftwood and enduring iron, and sailed down Fleet Ditch, "the roaring mother of dead dogs," to the City that hath foundations; the phrases ring still in my heart, noble music; worthier stuff than the prophecies of today — or should I say of yesterday? These, so far as I can make out, bid us abstain from meat and beer and tobacco, and the State shall give us a pound a day and save our souls alive. This message does not ring in my heart a noble music; I think Carlyle would have called it "a damned potato gospel." I read Carlyle, then, in my little room, and find a strange encouragement and strength in him. His picture of life is of a bitter struggle, and so indeed I find it — at twenty. Man, in Carlyle, is a poor wretch in thin and ragged clothes, out on a blasted heath, with all the heavens and all the clouds crashing and pouring upon him; blackness over him, hailstorms and fire showers his portion in the world. Get into whatever kennel or doghole you can find, says Carlyle, and shelter yourself from the blast so long as you can keep it, and be thankful. I liked the doctrine then, and it still seems to me a very good philosophy.

So I read and meditated night after night, and I am amazed at the utter loneliness of it all, when I contrast this life of mine with the beginnings of other men of letters. These others have often gathered friends of all sorts, both useful and pleasant, at the University; they have come of well-known stocks, every step they take is eased for them, their way is pointed out, there are hands to help them over the rough and difficult places. Or, even if they have not been at Oxford or Cambridge, if they have not come of "kent folk," they know, somehow or other, young fellows of their own age, with whom they can engage in endless talk about letters over eternal pipes and ever-welling tankards. One informs another, one, consciously or unconsciously, charts the other's way for him. I am often made quite envious when I see and hear how a young man, fresh on the town, drops so easily, so pleasantly, so delightfully into a quite distinguished place in literature before he is twenty-five. He enters the world of letters as a perfectly well-bred man enters a room full of a great and distinguished company, knowing exactly what to say, and how to say it; everyone is charmed to see him; he is at home at once; and almost a classic in a year or two.

And I, all alone in my little room, friendless, desolate; conscious to my very heart of my stuttering awkwardness whenever I thought of attempting the great speech of literature; wandering, bewildered, in the world of imagination, not knowing whither I went, feeling my way like a blind man, stumbling like a blind man, like a blind man striking my head against the wall, for me no help, no friends, no counsel, no comfort.

Somehow or other, out of a welter of reading of the most miscellaneous and shapeless sort, out of long

walks and long meditations, out of moonings and
loafings by Brentford and the parts thereto adjacent,
there rose up in the spring of 1883 the beginnings of
something that had a vague resemblance to a book. I
had finished that miserable "poem" which attempted
the manner of William Morris, and from that time my
attacks of verse-writing became brief and trifling, caus-
ing no uneasiness. And, this trouble happily over, I
became immersed in the study of scholastic logic, and
gave many days and nights to Whately's "Elements." I
got Thomson also, and dallied with the quantification
of the predicate, but I found such devices too new-fangled; what I wanted was the logic of the mediæval
schools, and in this I took a singular and intense
delight.

And here is a paradox, which may be worthy the
consideration of the curious: that age which was above
all the age of logic, was also the age of the most
luxuriant and splendid imagination. The scholars and
thinkers of the Middle Ages have been reproached with
idolizing the logical process to a point of utter extravagance, with treating the syllogism as a sort of divining
rod by which all the treasures of the spiritual, intellec-
tual, and physical worlds could be discovered and
drawn up from the dark womb and chaos of things
into the light of the sun. These reproaches, I think,
have chiefly proceeded from people to whom exact
thinking has proved unpleasant and unprofitable; but
it is certainly true that the logical art was deeply and
profoundly and constantly studied in the thirteenth
century — which was the age of the marvelous imagery,
the great magistry of the Gothic cathedrals, of the
Arthurian romances, of Dante. Nay, it is interesting to
note that Coleridge and De Quincey, two main agents
of the "renascence of wonder" at the beginning of the
nineteenth century, were both practiced logicians. It

would seem, therefore, that the dream and the syllogism have between them a certain secret alliance and bond, and so, naturally enough, two of the most extravagant dreams, "Alice in Wonderland," and "Alice Through the Looking-Glass," were the visions of a master of logic. As for the Snark, I can inform the inquisitive as to his true abode. He dwells in the place that is called Bocardo.

And so I steeped myself in these rare and entrancing studies, for such they seemed, and still seem to me. And thus I would sit on a bench on that bald, arid, detestable Shepherd's Bush Green, and be in reality, though not in actuality — let us for the moment adapt our discourse to the matter, and make the distinction — in cool, grey cloisters of the Middle Ages, walking in the silvery light with the Master of the Sentences, with the Angelic Doctor, listening to the high, interminable argument of the Schools. High, indeed, as dealing with immortal essences, not with monkeys' guts; interminable also in the manner of the cathedral rushing upwards to the stars which it cannot attain, of the old modes in which there are no true closes, but rather hints of undying melodies far beyond their endings; interminable, according to the dictum of one of these dark-robed Masters; *omnia exeunt in mysterium.* For there is a quest to which there is no term, nor bound, nor limit: *pelagus vastissimum.* Meditating these things, the jangling of the old horse trams might disturb me, and I would carry my quiddities to green fields by Hanger Hill, or to solitary places in Osterley Park, beyond Brentford, and so muse till the shadows came and sent me homeward under the twinkling, wavering lamps of those far-off days. Then for much tobacco, the disjunctive hypothetical syllogism and the strict rigor of the game. I am afraid very little of the old science has remained with me, but now and then

I come with some amusement on distinguished personages engaged in what they suppose is argument. I see no arguments; but undistributed middle terms are thick as October leaves in Wentwood.

From such a soil, then, the thing that had certain resemblances to a book rose up and gradually took shape, so far as it ever had any shape. It came up out of my logic books and out of Burton's "Anatomy of Melancholy," and so it was called "The Anatomy of Tankards." For, having enough sense, even though I was only twenty, to know that I could not write a serious treatise concerning the high doctrines that entranced me, I wrote a grave burlesque of what I loved. I examined into the essence of the tankard, I sought deeply into its quiddity, I divided its properties from its accidents, and distinguished again between the separable and inseparable accidents. I showed philosophically and conclusively that if there were no tankards there would be no men, that is, no rational or civilized men. For the ancient Greeks truly taught that man was raised from the brutish to the spiritual state by Bacchus, the giver of the vine. By wine is man made divine; and a diviner, says Bacbuc: and since wine must be contained before it can be drunk, it is clear that without tankards man cannot become divine; that is, cannot be man at all, in the proper sense of the term. And so on, and so on, with an infinite deal of easy dictionary learning, with much twisting of my logic formulæ; it was all too elaborate, elephantine, prolonged; a little thing that might have been well enough in its way drawn out into a big thing, and so spoiled. Still, I was only twenty, and twenty is apt to worry its bone long after all the meat has disappeared.

But if I could only have written the real book — that is, the dreamed, intended book — and not the actual book! Then, I promise you, you should have had high fantasies; not only arguments that began with a pebble by the way and rose upward to the evening star, that deduced all the shining worlds in an ineffable sorites from one mere letter of the alphabet. You should not only have been in at the death when Achilles caught at last the tortoise and passed him by, spurning his body into that utter void where parallel straight lines meet; you should have had an English Rabelais.

I remember taking my thoughts of the book up to Ealing Common one autumn evening. The work was drawing to a close, and I stood meditating the matter, looking from the height down towards Brentford. There was a wild sunset, scarlet and green and gold, and as it were, gardens of Persian roses, far in the evening sky. I stood by an old twisted oak, and thought of my book as I would have made it, and sighed, and so went home and made it as I could.

Chapter VI

The kind of life that I have been trying to indicate lasted for about eighteen months, and then my pupils mysteriously disappeared. Mysteriously, I say, for I

have completely forgotten what became of them, and
by what ways they left me. At all events, they vanished,
and I, being destitute, returned to Gwent and my old
home. There they were almost as poor as poverty, but
they were glad to see me. And I, waking in the morning
to the brave breath from the mountain, wandering in
the sunshine — it was summertime — about the gardens
and the orchards, revisiting the green, delicious heart
of the twisted brake, listening once more to the water
bubbling from the rock; I thought I had been translated from hell to paradise.

For, be it remembered, I have dealt gently with the
days of Clarendon Road. I have spoken for the most
part of the happier hours, of eager reading, of finding
an enchanting book on dusty shelves, on the delights
of the mind, on the capacity of changing dreary, common Shepherd's Bush into the cloistered walks of the
Schools, on the joy of obtaining some kind of literary
utterance. I have said little of the black days and the
waste nights, of the desolation that would sometimes
engulf me as it were with a deep flood. For many weeks
at a time I never spoke to any human being; save to
my pupils on Euclid and Cæsar, and this was a speech
that was no speech. And being born, I believe, with at
least the usual instincts of human fellowship and a
great love of all genial interchanges of thought and
opinion, this silence seared my spirit; to the interior
sense I must have shown as something burned and
blasted with ice-winds and fires. Indeed, when I was
released from this life in the manner that I have described, I came out, as it were, a prisoner from the black
pit of his dungeon, all confused, trembling, and afraid,
scarce able to bear the light of genial affection. For a
long while I spoke but little, and then with difficulty;
I was fast losing the habit of speech. Indeed, the eighteen months in Clarendon Road had been a very grave

experience; but I think that what affected my relations most in my demeanor was this: for a long time I would cut myself a piece of dry bread at tea, and munch it mechanically, having forgotten all about the use of butter. This struck them as dreadful; one might be poor, but to eat dry bread was more than poverty; it was beggary. When my aunt first noticed this trick of mine, she pushed the butter dish towards me, saying in a disturbed voice that there was no need for *that* anymore.

And for many days I was in a sort of swoon of delight. I had no desire for activities of any kind; I had all the happy languor of the convalescent about me. It was bliss to stroll gently in that delicious air, to watch the mists vanishing from the mountainside in the morning, to see again the old white farms beneath Twyn Barlwm and Mynydd Maen gleaming in the sunlight, to lie in deep green shade and to feel that I was at home again; that my troubles were over. I did not fret myself by inquiring as to whether they would not begin again. Indeed, in this first passion of relief, I loved to imagine myself as dwelling for the rest of my days amidst friendly faces in a friendly land, and devoting, say, fifty years to healing the wounds of eighteen months. It is a sorry thing to be but twenty-one and to feel so.

But it is thus, I suppose, that the man of the imaginative cast of mind pays, and pays heavily, for whatever qualities he may possess, and it will always be a question whether the price exacted be not too dear and beyond all proportion to the value received. But the case, I apprehend, is this: Mr. Masefield has said, very finely, that literature is the art of presenting the world as it were *in excess.* To the lovers in Mr. Stephen Phillips's drama of "Paolo and Francesca" the earth appears a greener green, the heavens a bluer blue; all beautiful things are raised to a higher power by the fire of their passion; the whole world is alchemized. And this state, which is a result of love, is the condition of imaginative work in literature, and so the man who is to make romances sees everything and feels everything acutely, or, as Mr. Masefield says, excessively. Now there would be nothing amiss in this state of things if these exalted and intensified perceptions could be utilized when there was a question of making a book and then abrogated and laid aside with pen and ink and paper. Unluckily, however, this cannot be so managed; and too often the dealer in dreams finds that his magic magnifying glass is tight fixed to his eyes and cannot be moved. And thus a mere common bore or nuisance appears to him as dreadful as Nero or Heliogabalus, the possibility of missing a train is as tragical as "Hamlet," and the pettiest griefs swell into the hugest sorrows.

I, in truth, had suffered; I had been through a dreary and a dismal experience enough; but my pains had racked me to excess; the pinpricks, unpleasant in plain earnest, had become stabs of a poisoned dagger. And so I came back to Gwent as to Avalon; there to heal me of my grievous wounds. So, as I say, it was mercifully given to me to saunter under the apple trees in July and August weather, to watch the sun and the wind on the quivering woods, to wander alone, and yet how deeply consoled and medicined, by the winding Soar Valley. Now and again I recollected, as I hope we shall recollect earthly torments in Paradise, as things over and paid for, the interminable, cruel labyrinths of London. I saw myself again, a half-starved, unhappy, desolate wretch astray in those intolerable, friendless, stony mazes of Notting Hill and Paddington and Harrow Road; I came again by obscene, obscure paths to Kensal Green, the place of the whited sepulchers.

Or the hideous raw row of suburban houses would suddenly confront me, surging up, a foul growth, from the green meadow, or the sick reek of the brickfields by Acton Vale blew in my nostrils. And the grim little room and solitude for the end of every journey!

I recollected these things, but though only days or weeks had been interposed between my happy state and my endurance of them they were as torments suffered in some remote æon. I said to myself, "I am as they that rest at last," and almost heard the words *In Convertendo*: with whatso in that psalm is after written.

*A*mong the books that I kept in my step-ladder library in Clarendon Road I mentioned that queer piece of sham learning and entertaining extravagance "The Rosicrucians: Their Rites and Mysteries," by Hargrave (or Hargreave?) Jennings. I said that this odd volume had eventually a curious influence on my life; and this was as follows: I was reading Herodotus and that portion of Herodotus which treats of Egypt — I have long ago forgotten the Muse which names the book — and Herodotus, it will be remembered, was very deeply interested in the Mysteries of the Egyptian religion. In treating of these occult things of Osiris the historian mentions certain singular matters which were highly pertinent to Mr. Jennings's thesis — if Mr. Jennings could be said to have had anything so definite as a thesis. But "The Rosicrucians" contained no mention of that which Herodotus had seen when night was on the Nile, so I ventured to write to the ingenious author, pointing out the particular passage which, I thought, would interest him. Mr. Jennings did not answer my letter; he was odd to extremity in most things, but in this particular he conformed perfectly to all the literary men whom I encountered in my early days. I came into contact with four or five men of a certain reputation; or perhaps I should say I came within sight of them; and they could very easily have flung me a word or two of encouragement, which would have been very precious to me then. But I never had that word, and so was forced to go on and do my best without it; the better way, no doubt, but a hard way. But though the author of "The Rosicrucians" did not reply to my letter, he passed my name and address to another man, a young fellow who had just set up as a publisher, and was going to issue one of the astounding Jennings books. So Davenport, the publisher, sent me his catalogue of new and second-hand books, and I, on reading it, sent him the manuscript of my "Anatomy of Tankards."

Here a parenthesis, if not several parentheses. We are now in 1884, and I had finished the "Anatomy" in the autumn of 1883. Soon after it was ended I sent the MS. to a gentleman who was then but in a small way. He is now a very eminent publisher indeed, and loved so much by his authors — by some of them at all events — as to be known as "Uncle." Well, "Uncle" (though, alas! it was not fated that he should ever be uncle-in-letters of mine) sent back the MS. in due season with a letter that almost made up for any disappointment my first "boomerang" may have occasioned.

His letter delighted me, not because it was specially complimentary, nor because it gave evidence of a careful and critical reading of the rejected manuscript, but because it was almost a replica of the publisher's letter which introduces Mr. Tobias Smollett's admirable epistolary romance, "Humphry Clinker." My actual publisher so resembled Smollett's feigned bookseller in the manner of his letter that I should suppose the one had deliberately made the other his model, did I not know

"Uncle" to be far too good a man to read such a book as "Humphry Clinker." I have not got my Smollett by me, I am sorry to say, so I cannot quote, but I may mention that both publishers made a very liberal use of the dash, or mark of parenthesis, and were curious in avoiding the word "I."

My letter ran somewhat as follows: —

"DEAR SIR,

"Referring to your favor of the 17th ult., enclosing MS. of work, 'Anatomy of Tankards' — have read MS. with interest — fear it would hardly command large sale — have had little encouragement to speculate lately — would recommend topic of more general public interest — hoping to have pleasure of hearing from you on some future occasion.

"ETC. ETC."

I was delighted, only a few years ago, to find that "Uncle's" hand has not lost its epistolary cunning. A distinguished friend of mine had been good enough of his own motion — not with my knowledge — to write to this publisher suggesting that a book by me would ornament his catalogue. The publisher approached me by letter. I wrote to him briefly, saying that I was just finishing a romance. He wrote back: "Sorry you speak of a romance — fear there is very little sale for those old things — however," etc. etc.

I did not trouble to go into whatever might lie beyond the portals of "however." But note the phrase, "those old things." It seems to me more precious than gold that has passed the furnace.

But to return from this backwater of narrative; I found Mr. Davenport established in an old street in the quarter of Covent Garden. I got to know this street well afterwards, and to like it, too, for all its associations and circumstances. Over the way, opposite to Davenport's offices, was the house where they said De Quincey had written his great book; there were theatrical shops all tinsel and wigs and grease paints close at hand, and on market days the street was all apack with carts and wagons and clamorous with marketmen who are still a rough and primitive and jovial race. Indeed, the market overflowed into York Street and submerged it, and I have had to leap over an undergrowth of green, springing ferns established on the office steps. Mr. Davenport had written me a very agreeable letter, and we had a very agreeable interview. The book on his publication-list which had attracted my attention was called "Tavern Talk and Maltworms' Gossip," and an admirable little anthology it was, compiled (as I found out afterwards) by Davenport himself. I thought there was a certain congruity between this book and my "Anatomy of Tankards," hence the dispatch of the manuscript to York Street. The publisher liked my book very much. He wanted to publish it badly; but there were certain preliminaries to be adjusted before this could be done, and I did not see how the obstacle could be surmounted. This conference took place at that singular hour of my career when my pupils seemed to melt away from me, as though they had been morning dew. I was just bound for the country, and the publisher agreed to hold the little matter of which I have spoken in suspense.

So I went westward, and there in Gwent there were kind people who had known my father all his days, and my grandfather before him, and so, for the sake of "the family," they helped me to arrange those "preliminaries." And, after all, perhaps it is fair enough that a man should pay his footing when he enters the craft.

So here was another element or elixir in the potion of my bliss, that I was drinking among those dearly-beloved hills and woods of Gwent. The bad old days were all over, and my torments were past; Clarendon Road and all its sad concatenations were like a black wrack of cloud seen far down on the horizon, as the sun rises splendid on a bright and happy day. I was come to the territory of Caerleon-on-Usk which was Avalon; and every herb of the fields and all the leaves of the wood, and the waters of all wells and streams were appointed for my healing. And my book was going to be published; I was to see myself in print, between covers — vegetable vellum they turned out to be — and I should be reviewed in London newspapers; and, not a doubt of it, be happy ever after.

Mr. Pecksniff, it will be remembered, spoke of the melancholy sweetness of youthful hopes. "I remember thinking once myself, in the days of my childhood, that pickled onions grew on trees, and that every ele-phant was born with an impregnable castle on his back. I have not found the fact to be so; far from it." Nor have I found "the fact" to be so. Still, these visions of fair print and title-pages and reviews are very pleasant in the green of youth, and they helped to make that summer of 1884 delightful for me. I "worked in" the thought of the coming proof-sheets — even the antici-pation of a proof-sheet is almost too much joy at twenty-one — into my escape from hard bondage, into the summer sunlight, into the odors of the solemn woods at night, into the cool breath of the brook, into the twilight fires of the sky above Twyn Barlwm. They were brave days while they lasted.

And now and again I had gallant tramps over the country with my old friend Bill Rowlands. I saw Bill a couple of years ago, after an interval of a quarter of a century, and Bill wore a long black coat and a solemn collar, having been a clerk in holy orders for many years. But when I began to speak of the little tavern at Castell-y-Bwch there was a twinkle in Bill's eye, and at the mention of the chimes of Usk, we both laughed till we cried — and perhaps we did cry internally. But I said to Bill, "Now I am going to take you to the Café Royal; it's the best I can do for you. But I wish it were the Three Salmons at Usk!" — where, if I remember rightly, we had bread and cheese and a great deal of beer and hot brandy and water to follow.

But that was a great day. We had gone over hill and dale, through the depths of woods and over waste lands, finding footpaths in the most unsuspected places that we had never dreamed of. And I remember that these footpaths gave me a singular impression of traveling in time — backwards, not forwards, as in Mr. Wells's enchantment. For the track of feet was but barely marked, and seemed on the point to fade away altogether, and the stiles that we climbed were of old, old oak, whitened and riven with age, and the outlets of these paths were into deep, forgotten lanes where no one came. And if one passed a house, it was roofless and ruinous; its gable-wall standing grey, with fifteenth-century corbel stones. The garden wall was fallen into a heap of stones, and the fruit trees were dead or straggled into wildness. So it seemed to me that we had fallen on old ways that were not of our day at all, and no one, perhaps, had been there for fifty or a hundred years, and if we saw anyone it would not be a man of our time. Bill, I am convinced, thought nothing of all this; his talk was of B.N.C. and mad tricks and all the mirth in the world, and I warmed the chilled hands of my spirit at his gaiety, as I had longed to warm my bodily hands at the watchman's brazier, glowing red in the cold London street. So Bill and I

came at last into Caerleon, having succeeded by much
extraordinary wandering in making five miles into ten,
and at Caerleon we drank old ale at the Hanbury Arms,
which is a mediæval hostelry, close to the Roman tower
by the river. And then nothing would satisfy us but to
go to Usk by the old road; again, ten miles instead of
five, but with our "short cut" imposed upon it, a good
fifteen miles.

The way goes over the river; on the right are King
Arthur's Round Table and the relics of the Roman city
wall of Isca Silurum, as the Second Augustan Legion,
garrisoned at Caerleon, called the place. Then through
the village, still known in my days as Caerleon-ultra-
pontem, and so into that most wonderful, enchanted,
delicious road that winds under the hillside, under
deep Wentwood, above the solemn curves and esses of
the river. We passed Bulmore, which does not mean a
moor of bulls, but pwll mawr, the great pool, of the
Usk river. It is a farmhouse now, but once a retired
officer of the 2nd Augustan had his villa here, and his
graveyard also: and here, I think, in the orchard, as they
were planting some young trees, they found the stone
inscribed: *Ave, Julia, carissima conjux; in æternum vale.*
Hail, Julia, dearest wife; farewell forever.

And here, to the best of my belief, Bill was telling
me how an undergraduate friend of his at B.N.C., a
schoolfellow of mine, found himself under the painful
necessity of screwing up the Dean in his rooms; the
screws employed being coffin-screws, headless, that is,
and not to be extracted without enormous pains.

We went on our way by the river, and passed under
Kemeys, a noble grey old house, with mullioned windows and Elizabethan chimneys. There is such a peace
about this place, such a sweetness from the wood, such
a refreshment from the water, so grave a repose upon
it, that I translated to Kemeys one of my heroes, a clerk

in Shepherd's Bush. This clerk had found out that all
the bustle and activity of modern life are delusions and
wild errors, and his reward was to be that he should
end his days at Kemeys, sheltered from all turmoil and
vanity, garnered from the evil world.

The peace of Kemeys was the peace of all the valley
of the Usk, and what balms it exhibited to my spirit
only those can know who have been bred in such
places, and have experienced the jar and dust and
racket of some great town, and then have returned to
the old groves.

My friend Bill and I went swinging along the winding lane beside the winding river, and as we went the
sound of pouring waters sang to us. For now the
overrunnings of the wells of Wentwood came from the
hill as rivulets, and about each stream its twisted
thicket grew, accompanying it all down the steep, to
the river below. We passed little Kemeys church, watching above the pools of the Usk, and then on the
hillside, almost in the shadow of the forest, was
Bartholly, that solitary house which awed me for years,
so that I made my awe into a tale. And here was
Newbridge, crossing a river that had now ceased to be
tidal and yellow, and had become glassy clear, and so
on northward, and it seemed into silences and solitudes that grew ever deeper and more solemn, more
evidently declaring the great art-magic of God that has
made all the world. The day drew on, the sun sank
below wild unknown hills — neither of us had ever
been this way before — and the green world was dim
for a while, and then was lighted up with the red flames
of the afterglow. The evening redness appeared, and in
those fires the ash tree became of immortal growth, the
round hills rose above no earthly land, the winding
river was a færy stream. Then, veil upon veil rising from

the level, rising from the fountains in the wood, mists closing in upon us.

My friend Bill said we should never get to Usk at this rate; he felt sure that there must be a short cut across the fields. So we took the first stile that appeared and set out over country that was utterly unknown to us; and the marvel was that we ever got to Usk at all — or to anywhere for the matter of that. I have a confused recollection of walking for hours in a gathering darkness, through jungles and brakes of dark wood, climbing hills that rose fantastic as out of dreamland, going down into dusky valleys where white mist rose icy from the courses of the brooks, threading an uncertain way through quaking marshland, and the regions of the distance as vague as shapes of smoke.

The bells were ringing nine when we came out of this dim world into Usk, and to the lights and cheerfulness of the Three Salmons, to ale and to laughter. There was a wonderful old fellow, a Water Bailiff, making the mirth of that cheerful, ancient parlor; and he told us of the tricks he had played on poachers and fishermen till we roared again. He was a fellow of strange disguises; if one of his stories were to be believed he had caught the most famous salmon poacher of the Usk by assuming the gait and utterance of a calf seeking for its mother at midnight. The tale may have been true; it was certainly an excellent entertainment.

Such was one of our days; and again we would go wandering over the mountains to west and to northward; climbing up into great high wild places of yellow gorse and grey limestone rocks, stretching and mounting onward and still beyond, so that one said in one's heart "forever and ever. Amen." High up there; the sunlight on that golden gorse, on the yellow lichens that encrusted the rocks ringed in old Druid circles, the great sweet wind that blew there, the heart of youth that rejoiced there, all the dear shining land of Gwent far below us, glorious; it is all an old song.

And there was a day on which we mounted over Mynydd Maen and came down into a valley in the very heart of the mountains, and walked there all the day, and in the evening returned again over the mountain at the southern end, winding under Twyn Barlwm as the twilight fell. It is only music, I think, that could image the wonder of the red sky over the færy dome, and the gathering dusk of the night as it fell on the rocks of that high land, on the streams rushing vehemently down into the darkness of the valley, on the lower woods, on the white farms, gleaming and then vanishing away. Only by music, if at all, can such things be expressed, since they are ineffable; not to be uttered in any literal or logical speech of men. And if one looks a little more closely into the nature of things it will become pretty plain, I think, that all that really matters and really exists is ineffable; that both the world without us — the tree and the brook and the hill — and the world within us do perpetually and necessarily transcend all our powers of utterance, whether to ourselves or to others. Night and day, sunrise and moonrise, and the noble assemblage of the stars, are continually exhibited to us, and we are forced to confess that not for one moment can we proclaim these appearances adequately. We stammer confusedly about them, much as a savage who had been taken through the National Gallery might stammer a few broken sentences, the applicability of which would be more or less dubious. "Woman — very bright round head," might be the Blackfellow's "description" of a famous Madonna; and a Turner would be summed up as "plenty clouds — one big tree." And in like manner we, confronted, not only with things remote and majestic, but with things familiar and near at hand, stutter a few lame sentences, endeavoring to describe what we have seen. And thus all literature can be but an approximation to the truth; not the "truth" of science, for that is a figment of the brain, a non-existent monster, like dragons, griffins, and basilisks; but to that truth which Keats perceived to be identical with beauty. And it is further evident that even this approximation to the truth of things is a matter of the utmost difficulty and not very far from a miracle, inasmuch as in a generation of men there are only two or three who achieve it, who in consequence are hailed as men of the highest genius.

Of course, there are persons for whom "truth" implies "even gilt-edged securities slumped heavily," or some such statement. To them, I tender my sincere apologies.

*T*he proof-sheets of my book began to appear early in that autumn of '84; they made me rapturous reading. And while I was correcting them, with a vast sense of the importance and dignity of the task, Davenport, the publisher, was writing to me, asking if I had any ideas for new books, and throwing out suggestions of his own.

Now this was very pleasant, for it all tended to persuade me, in spite of any doubts and fears of mine, that I was really a literary man. I would read Davenport's letters again and again, and deliberate gravely with myself over the answering of them; I enjoyed this very much indeed. But the correspondence led to no practical result; because I could not then — or ever — perform the Indian mango trick. The expert conjurers of the East, as is well known — in magazine fiction — will put a seed into a flower pot, cover up for a second

or two, and lo! there is a little plant. Again the conceal-
ment; the plant has grown, and so forth, till within the
space of five minutes you can gather ripe mangoes
from the tree that you saw sown. This is the mango
trick of fiction; that of fact, as I have seen it, is about
the dreariest and most ineffective piece of conjuring
imaginable. But, as I say, I could never imitate those
fabled Orientals. If Mr. Murray and Mr. Longman were
to jostle one another on my doorstep, clamoring for a
masterpiece, and offering Arabian terms, it would
make no difference; if I had no book within me, I
should not be able to produce one on demand. In
practice, I have found that I take about ten years to
grow these things; though I have one in my mind now
that was first thought of in 1898–99 and is not yet
begun.

So Mr. Davenport's letters produced no literature,
interesting though they were; and I must say that a less
sluggish mind would have found them stimulating in
a high degree. But the literary publisher struck on cold
iron; he suggested, I remember, a volume of scathing
criticism — "like Mozley's Essays" — as likely to receive
his most favorable attention. But, really, I could not
think of anybody that I particularly wanted to scathe
— now, perhaps, I could oblige a publisher in search
of anathemas and Ernulphus curses — and I had not
read Mozley, nor have I read him to this day. Then I,
on my side, suggested a book to be called "A Quiet
Life," this being, in fact, a description of the life that
I was then gratefully and gladly leading. I sent a speci-
men chapter, and so far as I remember Davenport
counseled me to defer the writing of *that* sort of book
till I was eighty or thereabouts. I daresay he was right.
Then my half-dozen copies of "The Anatomy of Tankards" reached me; and I believe that as soon as I saw
the book printed and complete in its (vegetable) vel-

lum boards I began to be ashamed of it. I think that this was hard lines, but the trick has been played on me again and again; and I do believe that a moderate, not excessive, dose of the good conceit of oneself is one of the chiefest boons that parents should beg from fairy godmothers for their offspring. For life is necessarily full of such buffetings and duckings, such kicks and blows and pummelings, that balms and elixirs and medicaments of healing are most urgently indicated, and there is nothing equal to this same rectified spirit of conceit. It may tend to make a man an ass, but it is better — or more agreeable, anyhow — to be an ass than to be miserable.

Then came the reviews, and they did me some good, for, as far as I remember them, they were kindly and indulgent. I think the critic of the "St. James's Gazette," then in its glory under the editorship of Greenwood, spoke of "this witty and humorous book," while he said, with absolute justice, that I had ruined the popularity of my parodies by their prolixity. Then the publisher, despairing, I suppose, of getting any ideas out of me, produced a notion of his own. He sent me three or four French texts of the "Heptameron," and bade me render it into the best English that I had within me; and so I did forthwith, for the sum of twenty pounds sterling. I wrote every night when the house was still, and every day I carried the roll of copy down the lane to meet the postman on his way to Caerleon-on-Usk.

And so my story has come round full circle. In the first of these chapters I told how the kindly speaker at the Persian Club, praising my version of the French classic, transported me in an instant from that shining banqueting hall in the heart of London, over the bridge of thirty years, into the shadows of the deep lane. Again it was the autumn evening, and the November twilight was passing into the gloom of night. There was a white ghost of the day in the sky far down in the west; but the bare woods were darkening under the leaden clouds; the familiar country grew into a wild land.

And I, with time to spare, walk slowly, meditatively down the hill, holding my manuscript, hoping that the day's portion has been well done. As I come to the stile there sounds faint through the rising of the melancholy night wind the note of the postman's horn. He has climbed the steep road that leads from Llandegveth village and is now two or three fields away.

It grows very dark; the waiting figure by the stile vanishes into the gloom. I can see it no more.

THE END

www.ingramcontent.com/pod-product-compliance
Lightning Source LLC
LaVergne TN
LVHW011244080426
835509LV00005B/619